schooled

schooled

Ordinary, Extraordinary Teaching in an Age of Change

Anne Lutz Fernandez
Catherine Lutz

Foreword by Ann Lieberman

TEACHERS COLLEGE PRESS

TEACHERS COLLEGE | COLUMBIA UNIVERSITY
NEW YORK AND LONDON

Published by Teachers College Press, 1234 Amsterdam Avenue, New York, NY 10027

Library of Congress Cataloging-in-Publication Data

Fernandez, Anne Lutz.
Schooled--ordinary, extraordinary teaching in an age of change / Anne Lutz Fernandez, Catherine Lutz ; foreword by Ann Lieberman.
      pages cm
Includes bibliographical references and index.
ISBN 978-0-8077-5736-9 (pbk. : alk. paper)
ISBN 978-0-8077-5737-6 (hardcover : alk. paper)
ISBN 978-0-8077-7432-8 (ebook)
      1. Teaching–United States. 2. Teachers–United States. 3. Public schools–United States. 4. Education--Aims and objectives–United States. 5. Educational change–United States. I. Lutz, Catherine. II. Title.
LB1025.3.F468 2015
371.102–dc23   2015014227

ISBN 978-0-8077-5736-9 (paper)
ISBN 978-0-08077-5737-6 (hardcover)
ISBN 978-0-8077-7432-8 (ebook)

Printed on acid-free paper
Manufactured in the United States of America

22   21   20   19   18   17   16   15   8   7   6   5   4   3   2   1

For Paul and Matt

contents

foreword

In the current educational context in the United States, teachers are being blamed for the problems in schools and for America's poor place in international test rankings. *Schooled* attempts to create an alternate view–one that focuses on the ideas and experiences of teachers–through the voices of nine fine teachers in all kinds of schools across the country. These "ordinary, extraordinary" people care passionately about teaching their students, whether rich or poor, or highly gifted or struggling.

Authors Anne Fernandez and Catherine Lutz interviewed teachers to find out what actually goes on in classrooms in all kinds of contexts. What they found is the tremendous disconnect between the real problems that teachers face, such as growing poverty, and the many solutions, such as increased standardized testing, being applied to solve these issues. What the teachers talk about–regardless of context–is the growing complexity of teaching. What we see in the teachers' schools and hear in the teachers' remarks is a set of challenging socioeconomic forces that affect classroom life. What we learn is teachers' incredible work in connecting academics to socioemotional problems, even as current reforms place restrictions on enacting these core necessities for being a good teacher. Reforms turn out to be "one size fits all" even as we learn of the complexities and realities of the lives of students, which demand greater teacher time, attention, and interpersonal savvy alongside their academic work.

A teacher in a Catholic school works with half of her students qualifying for a free or reduced lunch as per pupil spending has dropped and segregation increased, but gets striking engagement from her students in values-oriented discussions. We see a high school science instructor teaching about climate change in a political climate that favors creationism. We learn about a teacher in a magnet school focusing on STEM (science, technology, engineering, and mathematics) working hard to serve special needs students even as an overreliance on test prep and test scores takes time from teaching and learning. We get a glance at parents becoming teachers as they home school their children, many concerned with what they deem a poor school environment (drugs, peer pressure, academic instruction not to their liking). A teacher in a wealthier district where there are fewer discipline problems, higher pay, and better working conditions also has a reduction of support. Teachers take on additional duties in the school and have less time to collaborate with and learn from their colleagues, yet they work to support each other. In a former agricultural community, we follow a math teacher who works with an incredibly diverse array of students (who speak Tagalog, Arabic, Burmese, and Spanish). The focus of this school is cultural literacy and parent involvement using advances in technology. The diversity and poverty of the students, and multitasking required by teachers, do not deter good teaching. At a high school on an Indian reservation, we learn how a teacher struggles to maintain the values of the Reservation (wisdom, generosity, respect, courage) even as more than half of the population is below the poverty line and there is massive unemployment. Our understanding is broadened when we meet a high school teacher who has been teaching for 26 years who loves teenagers and loves the content that he teaches, while working creatively to add reading time and increasing screen time in his students' lives.

The writing in *Schooled* is so good that readers will be immediately involved in wanting to learn about schools, teachers, and students and what it takes to create healthy learning environments for the adults as well as the students. They will also see very clearly that we need to change our narrow test-driven reforms and support teachers in schools, providing them with the respect that other countries (Finland, Singapore, Canada) have found creates a healthy profession, where rather than leaving the job, people want to become teachers because it is a way to deal with both academic content and the social and emotional lives of their students. Think about the insightful questions for discussion in every chapter and take advantage of the suggestions for further reading.

This book makes an important case for defying the standardization that passes for school reform. We learn, first-hand, what it means to teach with passion and talent in a changing social, cultural and political environment.

–Ann Lieberman,
Senior Scholar at Stanford University

acknowledgments

We have many thanks to give.

Our greatest goes to the 9 teachers profiled here, all of them inspiring educators dedicated to helping children thrive. They generously agreed to share their time and thoughts in this book.

Thanks to those who facilitated our search for teachers to profile, especially Bruce Anderson, Tony Desnick, Jordan Kimball, John Willis, Holly Sulzycki, Tylee Jo Williams and Troops for Teachers, and Jo-Anne Jakab.

Thanks to the administrators who opened the doors to us at Cathedral Academy, EXPO for Excellence Elementary School, Gilbert High School, Jack Swigert Aerospace Academy, Liberty Charter School, Litchfield Park Elementary School, and William Fremd High School.

Thanks to our thoughtful, encouraging editor, Emily Spangler, at Teachers College Press, and to our supportive agent, Ellen Levine at Trident Media Group.

Thanks to Anne's colleagues in Westport, Connecticut, especially Julia McNamee, and to Catherine's friends Nora Huvelle and Lila Abu-Lughod. Thanks to Louie Montoya and Anna Shapiro for expert research assistance.

And thanks to family, especially sisters Mary Fox, Karina Lutz, and elementary teacher Elizabeth Lutz, who has profoundly influenced hundreds of Pennsylvania students; to Jonathan, Lianna, Liliana, and Maya; to our parents whose admiration for teaching and learning was communicated early and often; and to our husbands, fellow teachers whose love and work inspires us.

introduction

America's teachers: They are the nearly 4 million professionals who educate this country's young people, getting to work each morning in a kaleidoscopic array of classrooms, from regional public high schools down Arkansas roads to charter elementary schools aside Los Angeles freeways to Catholic middle schools near Florida's gated communities. They have been teaching for months or for decades, as a first or second career, on the path to principal or planning a lifetime in front of a whiteboard. Each has chosen to teach for highly individual reasons. Yet out of this multiplicity of school settings, personal histories, and professional motives, two images of teachers haunt, and limit, the discussion of education today.

In one, teachers are incompetents unqualified for better work, slackers who punch the clock of a short workday and spend long summers in hammocks, while draining public coffers and resisting every education reform. In the other, they are self-sacrificing, charismatic spitfires who inspire greatness in their charges by day, grade papers into the night, and single-handedly lift poor neighborhoods into the middle class. Portrayals of teachers in today's education policy climate range from desperately unflattering to wildly unrealistic; they're rarely more than cartoonish.

These contradictory stereotypes have emerged out of a driving narrative that the nation's education system is, simply put, a disaster—and that those who teach our children are overwhelmingly responsible for the mess. In the past few decades, *the* problem of education has been identified as bad teachers, rather than, or in isolation from, distorted national spending priorities, the challenges students face at home, or the insufficient rewards that society accords teachers. This narrative runs counter to most Americans' experience with their own or their children's teachers: The great majority of parents polled say their local schools and teachers are doing an excellent or good job. An unrelenting focus by politicians and the media on what's wrong with schools, however, leads roughly half as many to rate the nation's schools highly.[1] This drumbeat has also set the political climate for sweeping, one-size-fits-all educational reforms across regions, states, districts, and schools with very different cultures, strengths, and difficulties.

Ham-handed critiques of teachers are damaging a profession in which turnover is already high. Estimates of the long-term attrition rate for new teachers range from 20 to 40%, depending on the state.[2] On top of this,

1

several million veteran teachers expected to retire in the next decade will need replacing.[3] Who wants a hard job, though, that onlookers deem easy? Who wants a career requiring advanced degrees but paying a salary necessitating second jobs? Who wants work requiring great talent and technical skill that is dismissed as the backup plan for those who "can't do"? To avoid a recruitment crisis, more young people and career changers will need convincing that teaching is socially valued and personally rewarding.

Stereotyping teachers also works to sideline them from key conversations about education. While a handful of K–12 teachers have become media heroes and are occasionally invited to speak on behalf of the rest, there's been a lot more talking about teachers than talking with them. One study found that only 9% of guests invited to discuss education on cable news networks were educators.[4] Yet attempts to improve American education where it is lacking depend on the motivation of our dedicated teachers and on a willingness to tap into their expert knowledge about their students and about what works–and doesn't work–in teaching.

*   *   *

So who are America's teachers really? First and foremost, they constitute the nation's largest workforce. Our biggest employer is not Walmart, Microsoft, or the military; it is our network of schools, public and independent. Including students and all staff, one in five Americans enter a school each day, where they engage in our biggest national endeavor: educating the next generation.[5]

This enterprise's line workers are its 3.7 million teachers, and they are overwhelmingly women. Long female dominated, teaching is becoming more so: 84% of U.S. teachers today are women.[6] Despite high unemployment after the Great Recession and attempts to recruit men through alternate routes, the percentage of teachers who are male has been cut in half over the past quarter century.[7]

Many teachers work in institutions unlike the ones they attended. Twentieth-century America essentially had two kinds of schools, public and independent, situated in three basic environments: urban, suburban, and rural. Recently, school types have proliferated to include approximately 6,000 alternative schools, 5,700 charters, 3,000 magnets, 2,000 special education schools, and 1,500 vocational schools.[8] Ten percent of students attend independent schools, including Catholic, evangelical Christian, and other religious schools.[9]

America's schoolchildren are more ethnically diverse than ever as a result of the recent great wave of immigration, the second largest in the country's history. Despite this, individual teachers likely work with groups less heterogeneous by class and race than they would have taught in the 1970s, because of a slow resegregation of schools. And while the profession is diversifying, plenty of students see someone at the front of the classroom who does not look like they do: Eighty-four percent of teachers are White.[10]

Sprawl has blurred lines between cities and suburbs, between exurbs and country. While the national media focuses intensely on urban schools, less than one-third of America's teachers work in cities. One-quarter work in rural areas, and the rest work in towns of radically different sizes, geographies, economies, and demographics.[11] And more and more teaching is going on outside schools: Parents now educate 1.8 million children at home.[12]

Although the average required or contracted workday is 7 hours and 20 minutes long in U.S. public schools, American teachers report working an average of 53 hours weekly. They spend extra time before and after school on site and at home and engage in a range of activities, from tutoring students to grading assessments to emailing parents.[13] Because teachers earn relatively low salaries, many work second jobs to make ends meet. One recent report found that many midcareer teachers heading families of four or more were eligible for social service programs for the needy.[14]

Yet they are highly educated people, with 56% holding at least a master's degree. Clearly, many teachers could earn more doing something else. They choose the profession for an array of reasons that tend to be quite personal, yet overall they teach for one basic reason: They enjoy it. The majority of those surveyed say they are very or somewhat satisfied with their jobs.[15] This satisfaction, derived from relationships with students, parents, and other teachers, is threatened, however, by countervailing pressures: Teachers are less than thrilled with their pay, status, and—despite public perception of tenure—job security. As a result, the percentage of teachers reporting high satisfaction with their jobs is the lowest it's been since the 1980s.[16]

* * *

Whether cast as heroes, villains, or victims, America's teachers find themselves at the center of a sometimes ugly debate, one that can pit them against each other: tenured versus nontenured, young versus old, Black versus White, union versus nonunion, traditional versus charter school. Yet, while politicians, reformers, union bosses, and pundits contribute to the cacophony that serves as our national conversation about education, the voices of those who teach our children daily are barely heard. For this reason, we wanted to gather and share the views of working teachers on some of the key problems under debate—student motivation, college and career readiness, and the achievement gap among them—and some of the controversial solutions being applied to these, such as revamped teacher evaluations, curricular standardization, and increased testing. And because much modern education reform is based on presumptions about what motivates teachers, we wanted to understand *why* they teach.

So we set out to find teachers to talk to. Our goal was to identify a range of individuals—from various regions; in public schools and private academies; early in careers and near retirement; in city, town, suburb, and country—to report from the frontlines of teaching across diverse contexts.

As a high school teacher interested in the daily realities of education and an anthropologist interested in the complexities of culture, we didn't want to cherry-pick a collection of miracle workers from whom America's teaching force would be expected to receive wisdom. Believing that the ordinary work of teaching is extraordinary, we sought instead a more ordinary, extraordinary group: teachers who are competent, motivated, and thoughtful about their work. They weren't hard to find.

On social media, via friends and acquaintances, and through colleagues and education organizations, we put out a call that was answered by teachers from Connecticut to California. Despite working in highly social environments, teachers are paradoxically somewhat isolated from other adults, their work only partly visible to parents, the community, and other educators. As a result, we found many who relished the opportunity to discuss their work. More reluctant were home schooling parents, who can feel even more poorly treated by the media than do schoolteachers—yet because they are one of the fastest-growing groups of educators, we thought they should be part of the conversation. Ultimately, we screened, via email or phone, dozens who offered to be profiled or were recommended to us, choosing from these a mix of nine teachers who would allow us to see teaching in the widest range of schools and communities and whose personal histories were especially compelling. Although men disproportionately volunteered, we selected just two in order to reflect the profession's gender balance.

The teachers included in *Schooled* are neither typical nor outliers. Although they cannot be called representative of the larger group of nearly 4 million American teachers, each possesses a unique authority to speak on a specific set of educational issues. They include women such as Glorianna Under Baggage of South Dakota's Pine Ridge Reservation—where graduation rates are the nation's lowest—on the topic of dropout prevention, and men such as Robert Lewis, a special education teacher at a Colorado middle school and the father of an autistic son, on standardized testing of special-needs children. Their goal and ours is to open a discussion that values the perspective of classroom teachers. And indeed their thoughts on such critical issues provide insight for not just educators but anyone interested in American education.

In their schools, their homes, and their communities, we heard these teachers say and saw them show much more about their thinking and practice than surveys of thousands would provide. Our visits included interviews in which we explored their professional motivations and experiences, challenges and joys, educational philosophy and methods, and reflections on the profession and the state of education. We observed them in their classrooms and communities, where we were able to witness them at work with students, parents, and colleagues. (Note that the names of schoolchildren in our profiles have been changed.) As fellow teachers rather than investigative reporters, we found our conversations with the 9 had an easy, supportive quality that allowed us to go quickly to the honest and open core of their ideas about education.

On our journey we found, regardless of school setting, a significant disconnection between the problems teachers face in the classroom and some of the solutions that federal, state, and local authorities are rolling out to tackle them. We also discovered important differences between the goals of much modern reform and the fundamental purposes of education as many teachers see them. On the whole, the teachers in *Schooled* take the long view. They see the ultimate purpose of education not as the instruction of children but as the creation of adults. Consequently, they see academics as a means to an end, not the end itself. They see their roles as preparing students for college or career, yes, but even this is a means to an end: the production of socially competent, productive citizens who fulfill their potential. Where teachers vary in interesting and necessary ways is in the particular kind of adult they hope to help create; for one this might be a collaborative global citizen, for another an intellectual innovator or spiritual traditionalist.

Although teachers have found themselves attacked politically at various periods throughout the American past,[17] in this unique historic moment, their ability to deliver on their values is under threat from two sides. On one side, broader social and economic changes are making teaching harder. The list is long: widespread and increasing child poverty, widening income inequality, growing cultural and linguistic diversity, rising rates of children with disabilities, frequent school violence, limited job opportunities and ballooning college costs, contracting public budgets, and persistent racism and segregation. All are sharply felt in the classroom. The most profound of these factors are the basic economics; astoundingly, roughly half of America's public school students come from households without enough resources to sustain themselves.[18]

On the other side, education reform efforts at the national and state levels have led to new, often scripted curricula demanding less creativity, ever-changing pedagogical methods and technologies, more standardized testing interrupting learning, a fixation on collecting quantitative data on multifarious elements of teaching and learning, convoluted, even dysfunctional teacher evaluation programs, and declining professional prestige and stagnant compensation. Many teachers emphatically feel their autonomy is being constrained by cookie-cutter approaches and misdirected top-down reforms that devalue and disallow the full exercise of their professional craft—the art and science of teaching. This wasn't true just over a decade ago; before the No Child Left Behind and Race to the Top federal initiatives, teachers exercised a good degree of control over curriculum and instruction.[19] Yet if we reduce teachers to an academic delivery system, they are unlikely to achieve either the broader, long-term goals they aspire to reach or the narrower, short-term goals they're pressured to achieve: The glacial rate of improvement in national test scores in reading and math over the past decade is evidence of the latter.[20]

Schooled's teachers are responding in various ways to this pincer movement of challenging socioeconomic forces and constricting reforms. When they find them consistent with their educational philosophies, teachers are adopting, even embracing, reform strategies and tactics. South Carolina's Lisa Myrick, for example, a believer in interdisciplinary approaches, is adding lessons on nonfiction reading strategies from the Common Core State Standards to her chemistry curriculum. Such teachers are applying methods they might have employed anyway; none are resisting reforms they recognize as leading to good or improved teaching. At the other extreme, some are opting out of the system altogether, finding it untenable. Ohio home schooling parent Heather Frantz pulled her daughters from school when she saw how little individualized attention they were receiving. And within months of our visit, new teacher Lindsey McClintock left the Arizona classroom in which we saw her take 3rd-graders through scripted lessons, to enter private counseling, where she hopes to provide children with the social–emotional component being stripped from teaching.

And in the vast middle, teachers are working hard to hold on to what they know is good pedagogy. At times they are holding on quite desperately, with some, as one educator put it, "sneaking [in] a lot of good teaching under the table." Others, emboldened by their experience, reputation, tenure, or school climate, are more forthright and vocal in adhering to the strategies and methods they know work best. St. Paul's Ulla Tervo-Desnick, despite official cuts in recess, keeps on taking her 1st-graders outside multiple times a day to develop their physical and social skills. Gary Anderson of suburban Illinois devotes class time to independent reading despite the Common Core's push for teacher-led close reading instruction.

Americans worried about our schools have little to go on from the abstracted and vituperative political discourse about education. At the same time, teachers are subject to a flood of contradictory recommendations and directives, often from outside experts who seek to standardize education across communities that share great similarities but are marked by important differences. The nature of the profession makes it critical that teachers be empowered to live their pedagogical values and to address their students' needs. By opening the door to their classrooms and their lives, *Schooled's* teachers hope to show what they and their students actually experience, and they hope to inspire meaningful conversation about the complex challenges of teaching and learning in America today.

Ulla Tervo-Desnick

chapter 1

Teaching the Finnish Way in a World of Reform

(St. Paul, Minnesota)

Marcus had lost a tooth. He wasn't sure where or when, and, granted, it had been loose. But now he could run his tongue right through the gummy gap where that morning he'd jiggled it. His fellow 1st-graders were quieted so that Marcus, keeping a lid on his growing anxiety, could make this announcement and seek their help.

Within seconds, a team of two dozen pint-sized problem-solvers gathered on the classroom rug and started asking the slight, strawberry-blond boy some probing questions that might crack the mystery. They were bound by the shared understanding that without the tooth, Marcus might go unremunerated for one of the few assets that 6-year-olds hold. They were bound, too, by the knowledge that he would do the same for them. With the determination that raises barns, Miss Ulla's class at St. Paul's EXPO for Excellence Elementary *would find that tooth.*

Taking minutes out of a seam-busting school day to exploit a teachable moment like this is no longer easy for America's elementary school teachers. Although problem-solving, self-advocacy, teamwork, and other so-called soft skills are life and learning skills that have long been essential components of written and unwritten K–12 curricula nationwide, elementary teachers are now given innumerable directives to use every minute of instructional time for academics such as reading, writing, and math—even in 1st grade. Ulla Tervo-Desnick, though, shows it's possible to do both.

Ulla was born in Helsinki, Finland, and raised there by her father, an aeronautical engineer, and her mother, a high school literature teacher. A month of substitute teaching might convince most people to pursue any other line of work: lumberjacking, waste management, air traffic control. Yet a year of subbing after high school convinced Ulla to set aside other loves, including French and acting, to study teaching at the University of Helsinki.

She had not forgotten what the profession had taken from her mother in time and energy. Every afternoon when young Ulla got home from school, she would watch at the window. The moment she saw her mother coming from the bus stop, she would fire up the coffeepot to refuel her for the work to come: hours of tutoring, grading, and planning. But Ulla also remembered what teaching gave her mother in joy and fulfillment.

When we met at her house near where the Mississippi River cleaves the Twin Cities, it was a pot of tea Ulla put on to rejuvenate herself after the school day. Like her unpretentious home, Ulla has a bright and simple elegance. Her cropped hair is the perfect silver that gray always hopes to be, her makeup a quick tint of berry gloss, her neat cardigan accented with a scarf.

While her husband, Tony, prepared dinner, Ulla sat with us at her dining table and explained how a Finnish woman ended up teaching American children in Minnesota, and it had much to do with the bespectacled man in the kitchen baking our salmon. In the 1980s, Ulla Tervo met Tony Desnick, then an architecture student, on his European travels. A few years later, the pair reconnected and moved to Minneapolis, Tony's hometown, before settling in St. Paul.

When the couple were "shopping for schools" for their daughters, they felt fortunate to find the educational setting they were seeking only a mile and a half away, a new magnet called EXPO Elementary. "You could feel the creativity; you could feel the excitement," Ulla explained. "The children got to express themselves; they got to have fun. They were treated like children. It felt like it was a good place to learn." She was right. Her children thrived at EXPO. Then one day while she was volunteering there, a staff member asked if she knew any good candidates for an opening in 1st grade. Having recently completed the coursework for Minnesota certification, Ulla volunteered herself. That was 15 years ago.

Because they draw students from beyond a neighborhood's or even a district's boundaries, magnet schools were initially seen as a way to mitigate racial segregation in public schools, especially after many Whites fled cities in the 1960s and 1970s. The popularity of these schools, which were seen as a means of providing parental choice and encouraging educational innovation, grew through the 1980s and 1990s. Theme-focused magnets can offer a curriculum organized around subject areas such as technology or the arts. Historically, magnets have leaned toward student-centered instruction and inquiry-based learning and have housed exemplar programs for the gifted and talented; EXPO fit this model.[1]

When it opened in 1990, the school's mission was to "give children the tools and the skills to become citizens of the world, exploring, solving problems together, growing into active, engaged members of their communities."[2] This dovetailed exactly with Ulla's educational philosophy, one that emerged from her experiences training and working as a teacher in Finland.

Finland's education system, which underwent a slow, thoughtful, systematic set of reforms over several decades, has received considerable global attention as those changes have led to striking improvements. Remarkable repeat performances on international standardized tests and a narrow gap of achievement between its strongest and weakest students are two reasons why the country's educational and attendant economic transformations became known as "the Finnish miracle." Its chief missionary is the former head of Finland's Ministry of Education and Culture, Pasi Sahlberg, who spreads the gospel through his writing and at symposia worldwide.

In his book *Finnish Lessons: What Can the World Learn from Educational Change in Finland?*, Sahlberg details Finland's instructional focus on problem solving, cooperative learning, flexibility and individualization, experiential and hands-on learning, metacognition (learning about learning), and developing social skills and creativity. These are not a few things. They all flow, however, from a national consensus that education's purpose is to provide equal opportunity for all children to develop into independent, well-rounded individuals, a purpose that once achieved would lead to economic growth and social cohesion even as the population diversified. To teach this way instead of relying on direct instruction and prepackaged curriculum, the Finns understand, requires intelligent, committed professionals, so Finland skims the teaching pool off the top of each year's graduating college class, and then requires those future educators to obtain a master's degree before licensing.

She teaches, Ulla told us, to help children develop personally and socially as well as academically, and she does this by emphasizing empathy, collaboration, creativity, and problem solving. Sounded pretty Finnish.

Modern American education reform efforts, kick-started in 1984 with the dramatic release of the government report *A Nation at Risk*, have been spurred by the desire to better compete internationally. The United States has since continued to produce only middling results on international academic achievement tests, justifying aggressive state and federal reform measures.

So what would happen if you put a Finnish teacher in an American school in the era of reform? Through our conversations with Ulla and a day at EXPO, we hoped to find out.

* * *

With the exception of a 45-minute period when her students are at music or art and of a half hour for lunch, Ulla spends the day managing a classroom of 28 first-graders. Seventeen or 18 students per class was once typical for the early grades in St. Paul, but class sizes had recently ballooned.[3] Classroom aides, who help manage behavior and provide academic support, are a memory; they were lost with budget cuts, Ulla told us, 2 years earlier. At a few points during the day, selected students are pulled out to work with a parent volunteer or a reading specialist, but otherwise, as Ulla put it, she's "flying solo the whole day with kids. With lots and lots of kids." Still, it is with the light-handed control of a seasoned pilot that she takes her charges into flight each weekday, with take-off at 8:00 a.m. and a soft landing at 2:45 p.m.

On a cold, gray April morning, our taxi dropped us in front of EXPO's squat building, which sits in a neighborhood of modest single-family, single-car-garage homes in St. Paul's Highland district. Ulla welcomed us into her cheerful classroom a few minutes before the students started to arrive.

Student art mounted on construction paper hung from clotheslines criss-crossing overhead; maps and posters and calendars and charts and checklists plastered the walls; a bright-orange throw covered a comfy sofa in a reading corner. Candy-colored files stuffed with student journals and plastic buckets of art supplies stood stacked atop shelves bulging with books and games, a spinning globe topped a piano (a piano!), and in the center, blue stability balls serving as desk chairs surrounded six work tables.

We situated ourselves at a table on which clustered "owls" sat, made from paper cups, pantyhose, dirt, sprouting grass seed, and pasted-on googly eyes. The first students filtered into the room. Some had picked up bagged breakfasts in the lobby, evidence of a recent push to increase participation in Minnesota's school breakfast program. Three hundred thousand of the state's children qualify for the program, and though there is more affluence here than at many St. Paul schools, EXPO serves plenty of poor children who are underfed, overtired, or underdressed—and thus at a learning disadvantage from the get-go.[4]

More children arrived, located writing journals or books, hopped up on stability balls, and got to work chewing, writing, drawing, or reading. A few came escorted by parents who paused to chat with Ulla. Three boys gathered to greet each other and, like middle-aged managers at the watercooler, swap jokes (one with the punch line "Bring it on, fat guy" got the biggest laugh) before redirecting themselves to their morning tasks. A boy named James sidled by our table as much to check us out as to assess the growth of his owl's grassy locks.

Then, a moment that would make most parents weep: Without being asked, as they'd been taught to do from day one of the year, the children packed up their breakfast trash and deposited it in bins.

By 8:30, it was time for everyone to assemble on the rug in the front of the classroom. Miss Ulla sat at the piano and asked, "Does anyone want to do a solo today? Does anyone have a song in their heart?" The answer was yes, and as the volunteers popped up one by one, that song was almost always a fine ditty about geography ("Continents, continents, do you know your continents?") that allowed the vocalist to use the pointer on the world map. One girl with an especially strong voice brought some welcome variety with "Good Morning, Good Morning," and a boy sang hello in various languages.

After a final song together sung standing in a circle, they all stopped to shake hands with their neighbors—"Good morning, Mia!" "Good morning, Zach!" "Good morning, Allie!" "Good morning, Ned!" Then Ulla directed, "Put your finger on your nose if you looked in the other person's eyes" and "Put your hand on your head if it was the right kind of squeeze." The rest of this "morning meeting" provided an espresso shot of the soft-skill-getting, student-choice-giving activities Ulla would interweave throughout the day. Large numbers of American elementary schools have, like EXPO, adopted methods of the Responsive Classroom, such as its hallmark morning meeting, to encourage social and emotional learning, improve behavior, and provide a safe learning environment.[5] While these methods might appear to consume class time better spent on academic instruction, they have been shown to lead to higher academic achievement.[6]

Student behaviors spoke to these efforts. One boy raised his hand to remark sadly that he'd noticed that Lily, who'd been out sick several days, wasn't sitting in her spot in the circle, revealing how Ulla had built empathy and community. Ulla took advantage of the moment to review proper hand-washing technique, which seemed like excellent timing, since we soon learned from another solemn child that the day before, Andreas had "barfed" and gone home early.

Surprisingly, there were no giggles at the mention of Andreas's barfing, but if there had been, discipline would have been swift, gentle, and discreet. Each time that an infraction occurred, the errant child was directed to take a break on a chair at the side of the room. In every case, the short march was made on cue without wince, whine, or wheedle, the outcome of a focus on fostering responsibility and self-control.

The morning meeting closed with a read-aloud and a preview of the math lesson to come. For this, Ulla held aloft a slice of wheat bread and asked how it might be split. "How would you split it in half? In quarters? In eighths?" Thinking about how this concrete object might be shared would help make the lesson involving division less abstract.

Students then headed to their tables of four or five, where Ulla guided them in a hands-on lesson in which they cut squares from paper and figured out different ways to fold them to create two, then four, then more parts. Adam, struggling with the concept, received extra attention from Ulla, but he'd been having a tough day behaving and staying on task; he'd had to take several breaks. Now, frustrated that making two folds did not make two parts no matter how many times he tried—getting at the heart of the lesson—Adam was neither heeding advice nor observing how others were problem solving. Ulla, a bit frustrated herself, asked, "It seems like you're not trying today. Can you tell me why you are not trying?" The message was clear: Effort, not ability, was the key to success.

After math came recess, but it was raining cold and hard, and so the students recharged by playing indoor games instead. Ulla takes recess seriously. She rarely lets weather get in the way, making sure everyone has outdoor gear so she can continue to provide year round what most other district teachers have been forced to drop in favor of more academics. In Finland, younger children experience a shorter school day, which even then includes less work and more play. It frustrates Ulla that in St. Paul, a kindergartner clocks in as many hours as does a high school senior; whether it is developmentally appropriate or not, 5- and 6-year-olds must power through school days almost 7 hours long.

"For a Finn, that doesn't make any sense," she explained, because 5-year-olds have different needs from those of 18-year-olds. The Finnish system for the early grades is "based on play. It's based on lots of outdoor activity, hands-on activity. There is a lot of rest time." The academic content of a school day in Finland for a child of kindergarten age she estimates at 90 minutes, while in St. Paul it approaches 4 hours. By the time they are in high school and better able to sustain focus, Finnish children engage in a more rigorous course of study than do most American teens.[7] "Expectations start with the child, with what does the child need."

After a speedy cleanup, the games were neatly shelved and the class had regrouped on the rug. Ulla introduced a poetry unit by reading, in a lilting voice that would soothe a poked bear, a poem by Eloise Greenfield titled "The Daydreamers." While for other activities on the rug, the students must be seated, facing forward, and attending with eyes, ears, and "heart," now they could lie back and relax, and Ulla told them she would read the poem again. "This time, close your eyes. Just listen to the words. Then, when I am done, I will ask you to tell me any words that stuck in your head."

When she finished, the students opened their eyes and several raised their hands. *Daydream, hopscotch, dance, world*: These words took hold. Then Ulla asked, "Where do you like to go in your daydreams?"

Their imaginations broke free at this smallest permission: "a cave"; "the Bermuda Triangle"; "Bacon World"; "a place where there's art you can take off the wall and it comes to life"; "165 million years ago"; "China. No, Hawaii." This bit of brainstorming did the trick; flush with ideas for their writer's notebooks, they hustled to their tables. Ulla wrote a sentence starter on the whiteboard: "When I daydream, I _____." She turned on some low classical music, and each little head bent over. Words began to fly into their notebooks.

One girl started, "When I daydream, I dream that Miss Ulla is my mother."

After lunch, the students were presented with choices for indoor recess (the rain was turning to snow), and more than half opted for quiet reading. Some chose to participate in a yoga lesson led by a girl who instructed them in a new pose: "It's called the Eagle. I made it up myself." It wouldn't be the last time that day when students had a say in their activities, leading to nearly universal engagement. These children needed neither pushing nor prodding to stay on task. Student choice is Miss Ulla's cold hard cash, and she spreads it around judiciously but generously.

After this second recess, a parent volunteer pulled a small group for extra reading help, and Ulla put the rest to work practicing printing in workbooks or connecting jigsaw puzzle pieces to make grammatically correct sentences. Silly sentences such as "A banana jumped over a squirrel" were crowd pleasers when later shared aloud.

Meanwhile, Ulla called to the rug, in turn, each of five skill-level-based reading groups. While they read with her, she provided strategies and assessed their progress. In multiple ways it is a luxury to have so many gifted and talented children in a single classroom: They set the bar high and can help other students learn. But it's also not easy to make sure that the gifted students are challenged, that they can take leaps while others get needed scaffolding.

Ulla maintained that differentiation is the key to managing her heterogeneous and oversized class, but when pressed she admitted that despite her best efforts, with more students, "you just do less. You do less because everything takes longer. You add a child, and that child needs what any other child needs, so you just do less. You have to physically attend to everybody in so many different ways, especially the younger children, who need so much. They need assurance, they need contact, they *need*."

There are other reasons why the time and attention Ulla can devote to each student is getting pinched. This year, under a district directive, teachers are spending less time in the classroom so that they can spend more time working together. Typically, teachers would welcome time to collaborate with and educate one another, for example, by sharing successful lessons or tech how-to. A hallmark of the envied Finnish system is that teachers spend less time teaching and more time preparing to teach than do educators in other developed countries, including 2 hours weekly working with colleagues to shape local curriculum.[8] But this isn't that, by any means.

Instead, Ulla and her fellow 1st-grade teachers spend 2 hours a week collecting data, entering it into a computer, then reviewing it to determine if they met some goal—for example, how many sight words their students know. But Ulla argued, "If the focus of your time together is data collection, then the focus is data collection. It's not how to help this child or that child. So unfortunately we look at it as a missed opportunity." Ulla has hope that eventually teachers will be able to take more ownership of this time and put it to better use. For now, they submit their data to district administration, unsure how or whether anyone looks at it.

And in the classroom, there is more data to input. Those reading groups Ulla worked with? While meeting with each, she is supposed to log on to a program that provides the goal and materials for that group's lesson; after teaching the lesson, she is to check a box indicating whether the group met the goal, didn't meet it, or are still working on it. This practice is, naturally, impossible in a class of 28 living, breathing human children. If it were possible, it would likely hinder the flexibility that characterizes great teaching.

The trend toward micromanaging teachers pains Ulla, as it is antithetical to everything she knows from research and experience to be effective. She explained to us, as she does to community groups who invite her to speak about the Finnish system, "In Finland, there is just enormous autonomy given to teachers and schools. They get to make a lot of their decisions and figure out how to go about it. And if something doesn't go well, then it's the principal's responsibility to look into it and make changes." By contrast, here "we are very centrally controlled. More and more every year." A stronger teacher's union like Finland's could resist these trends, Ulla believes, but she sees St. Paul's union as weak.

*   *   *

Exhausted by noon though we'd only been observing, we asked Ulla if she ever considers working with children a bit more mature and independent. "I would move to a higher grade, but 1st grade still gives me a little bit of freedom to do the things that I see are right for kids. Because if I go to 3rd grade, there is testing. And I don't think I could feel good about my work if I had to follow those expectations. It just wouldn't be teaching for me anymore in the way that sustains me. I have to be able to make enough calls for me to make it my own. Otherwise, what's the point?"

By 3rd grade, Minnesota children, like their counterparts across the country, undergo a battery of standardized tests—assault and battery, some joke—to assess student learning. The Minnesota Comprehensive Assessments (MCAs) are administered to students annually from 3rd through 8th grade in reading, mathematics, and science; additional exams are given in high school. The results are used to evaluate districts, schools, teachers, and students, and they can affect the funding a school receives from the state.[9]

How these scores are used profoundly affects what teachers in these grades teach and how they teach it—math, reading, science, and seatwork will trump gym, art, and time-intensive hands-on projects—and this can alter the entire mission of a school and which students pass through its doors. One issue that MCA scores have highlighted is the gap between high and low performers in St. Paul and in individual schools. EXPO has an especially wide achievement gap,[10] which should be no surprise, since it attracts gifted children from all over the city, high-achieving students who share a school with special education students, whom it also serves well but who tend to underperform on standardized tests.

Based on this gap, however, Ulla explained, EXPO lost, at least temporarily, its magnet status, meaning it no longer qualified for busing. City parents who would like to choose EXPO can now do so only if they live within walking distance or can drive their children to school, limiting its socio-economic diversity.[11] EXPO might return, as other district schools have, to being a neighborhood school, further homogenizing the school population. Based on the neighborhood, the student body, already about a third non-White compared with three-quarters non-White for St. Paul, would Whiten further. In turn, the school's achievement gap would be expected to narrow. Problem solved!

Ulla fears EXPO is deviating in other ways from the mission that drew her as a parent and teacher to the school—since education reform efforts are often at odds with that mission. "It is the current educational climate. It seeps into the classroom. We try as teachers, we try at least at our school, to insulate ourselves from it, but it seeps in, and it's just harder to keep the standardization, the creeping of higher expectations at younger and younger ages, out. What used to be developmentally appropriate now isn't."

Ulla provided one telling example of how ideas about developmental appropriateness have changed. When 1st-graders write, they tend to print large letters and so can fill entire pages with just a few sentences. Historically at EXPO, if, even midway through 1st grade, a child had large handwriting, there would be little concern, based on the understanding that his or her skills would come along with time. Now, "red flags go up," and the child will be discussed at a "staff team" meeting, a precursor to a referral for special education services. Counterproductive stress is piled on teachers, parents, and children when normal differences between children are seen as deficits and become unacceptable.

Many of her St. Paul colleagues are, Ulla said, "sneaking a lot of good teaching under the table" despite the regimentation of a testing culture. And EXPO parents are grateful—after all, they chose the school for its reputation, built on its unique mission. Ulla carefully offered, "The district and the parents, I feel, sometimes want different things. The parents want a good place for their kids to learn where they can be children. But the district has a different model."

So, if she taught 3rd grade now, it would be harder for Ulla to "get away" with being the teacher she is and wants to be. And even staying with 1st grade, she might experience the encroachment of the testing culture, making it harder for her to help shape not just what her students know but also who they are. Fewer songs would be sung; fewer daydreams would be shared; fewer muscles would be stretched; fewer chances would be had to help others.

Which brings us back to Marcus.

In the midst of the conference on the rug, Marcus remembered last feeling the tooth in his mouth while at lunch. He was now convinced it was somewhere in the cafeteria. The problem was that the lunch period was over and the cafeteria closed.

"I'm just not sure how I'm going to be able to get in there without getting in trouble," he said, his tone of chagrin implying that gaining access to such a secure area might require the help of SEAL Team 6.

Ideas were bandied about. Then, with the bright confidence of a junior executive, Alex, a girl in a trim pageboy, announced, "I have a possible solution. Two kids could go with one of these teachers," pointing at the two of us sitting in the back of the room with seemingly nothing but time on our hands, "to the cafeteria to look for the tooth. That should work."

Everybody liked this idea. Miss Ulla asked Marcus to choose one student, who, along with Alex and the designated adult, would accompany him on his mission. Hands shot up. With the deliberation of a president making a cabinet appointment, Marcus made his choice, and the team headed off. When they returned, they would report success in getting into the cafeteria, failure in finding the tooth, and a queasy Marcus would conclude that he just might have had his tooth for lunch, along with his sandwich.

Questions for Discussion

- What can we learn from international comparisons of educational systems? What are the limitations of these comparisons?
- To what extent can teachers individualize learning, especially when class sizes are large?
- How can the health benefits of physical activity and the learning benefits of play be preserved in the face of growing academic demands in the younger grades?
- How important is it to teach collaboration, interpersonal, and other so-called soft skills in school?
- Can teachers resist the pressure to "teach to the test" when they and their schools are being evaluated and resourced in part based on test scores?

Suggestions for Further Reading

A Nation at Risk: The Imperative for Educational Reform. The National Commission on Excellence in Education. April 1983. http://www2. ed.gov/pubs/NatAtRisk/risk.html

Programme for International Student Assessment (PISA). Home page. Organisation for Economic Co-operation and Development. http://www. oecd.org/pisa/

Sahlberg, P. *Finnish Lessons 2.0: What Can the World Learn from Educational Change in Finland?* (2nd ed). (Teachers College Press, 2015).

Singer, D. G., Michnick Golinkoff, R., and Hirsh-Pasek, K., eds. *Play = Learning: How Play Motivates and Enhances Children's Cognitive and Social-Emotional Growth* (Oxford University Press, 2011).

Wagner, T. *The Global Achievement Gap: Why Even Our Best Schools Don't Teach the New Survival Skills Our Children Need—and What We Can Do About It* (Basic Books, 2010).

Ann Marie Donnelly

chapter 2

The Way, the Truth, and
To Kill a Mockingbird
Faith-Based Teaching in a Catholic Classroom

(Bridgeport, Connecticut)

Adamina approached the microphone before the audience of several hundred assembled in the gym. The 8th-grader's thick, raven hair was combed in a swoop across her forehead, draped low enough that her eyes were completely in shadow. From behind that shield of hair, she began in the most public way to perform her private thoughts, share her art, proclaim her identity:

I am different, but unique
I am weird and creepy
I am weak outside, but strong inside
I am a freak
I am a crazy pasta lover
I am bulletproof
I am a loner
I am silent. Silence is the most powerful scream
I am not perfect
I am a tunnel of sadness
I am a blank piece of paper waiting to be drawn on
I am a somebody
I am the one with a fake smile
I am in love with a corner
I am darkness waiting to be lit

As she finished, applause covered her in a wave of approval.

That day had begun as a brisk spring one, with fresh-faced children patiently lined up in rows outside Bridgeport's Cathedral Academy, on an asphalt parking lot that doubles, as in so many cities, as a recreation area for the pre-K–8 school. Their neat uniforms and the stolid gray masonry of the cathedral behind them suggested a timeless, orderly routine, though

21

the lives of this city and its children have often been turbulent. Neither would today be routine. Excitement was in the air; 8th-grade teacher Ann Marie Donnelly had organized an assembly to mark the culmination of seven weekly visits to the school by literature professors and students from Fairfield University, a Jesuit college nearby. During these visits, Cathedral teachers and students had studied poetry together, learning the difference between sensory and place poems, false apologies and praise poems, collaborative poems and self-portraits like Adamina's. Students seized the chance to create insights into their own lives through the creative and critical thinking these lessons prompted. In the weeks following the assembly, Ann Marie would produce a poem chapbook that the children were intensely proud to be included in as published writers.

Not all the work was as deep or dark as Adamina's. Hope radiated in a piece by a 7th-grader who celebrated being the only Colombian in his class: "I am the beat when the bass drops / The one that everyone loves / I am the future / Trying to forget the past / I am waiting in darkness / To become the light of the world." These two poets open small windows into the world of Ann Marie's students.

Ann Marie teaches English and history, and she twins the subjects each year in a research project on 20th-century history relevant to understanding the novel *To Kill a Mockingbird*. On a sheet of easel paper, Ann Marie had listed, with crisp Catholic school penmanship, her students' chosen topics alongside their names. As we scanned the list, noting that Jaylen was studying the civil rights movement and Aliyah the Kennedy assassination, Cameron came up to point out that he was researching the FBI. A number of boys had chosen crime-related topics such as the Mafia. Questions of ethnicity, race, violence, and the law, of course, resonate with *Mockingbird* but lead the children to learn about topics that transcend the particular time and place Harper Lee wrote about.

Ann Marie feels an obligation to raise questions of social justice in her classroom. Racism's realities, she thinks, have remained surprisingly invisible to many of her students despite their living in a context created in part by racism: Their neighborhoods and school are segregated from White Connecticut, from White America. At the same time, while Whites represent just 1% of the student body, her students live and learn in a world that is remarkably diverse, with their peers hailing from 25 or so different countries of origin. So, "they don't think of themselves as being a minority" or belonging to a category called "non-White." But this means, as Ann Marie sees it, that they live in a "bubble" into which racial animosity only sometimes intrudes.

When it does, it can be a shock. She has seen it happen at interdistrict basketball games: "They're playing against a team from suburbia, and all the kids on those teams are White. And truthfully are not really nice. They don't smack hands, they won't shake hands at the end of the game. One team spit on their hands [before smacking hands with] our kids. Our kids are like, 'What did we do?' They don't understand."

She went on, "Because we're so diverse, that's what they're used to, that's what they know." Focusing on the bright side, she believes her students are being better prepared for cooperation and understanding in the wider adult world than are their suburban peers growing up in a separate bubble. At the same time, she feels an imperative to prepare them for a future sadly bound in the past, even as America's racial achievement and income gap has narrowed: a future in which being a person of color still makes someone more likely to be un- or underemployed and less likely to get a college degree. In 2005, 62% of Whites and 40% of Blacks graduated from college within 6 years of matriculating.[1]

In part because few of her students' parents have had a college experience, Ann Marie tries to educate her 8th-graders about the path there. Some boys, expecting to be the next LeBron James, pin their hopes on a basketball scholarship, and so she uses March Madness as a teachable moment: She has each student pick the name of a competing school out of a hat and research the college's cost and requirements for admission and aid.

Ann Marie has been working in the same room in the same building for 28 years, for the most part teaching middle schoolers. Her work extends outside, however, as she taps into community resources, such as bringing in those college poetry teachers or providing students the opportunity to act as docents at the local art museum. Scrambling for resources is part of the job of teaching in the city's public and parochial schools.

American teachers spent an average of $513 of their own money on class supplies, teaching materials, and professional development in one recent year.[2] They increasingly turn to crowdsourcing sites such as DonorsChoose, which raised nearly $57 million for public schools in just one recent year.[3] Teachers also join parents in a crush of school fundraising efforts—bake sales, carnivals, product sales, raffles, and auctions—that annually raise untold millions, perhaps even billions. These efforts were once more modest, covering only extras like field trips. They now go toward funding such basics as capital improvements, art and music classes, and textbooks. Fundraising campaigns accelerated as 34 out of 50 states allowed per pupil spending in 2013–2014 to drop below 2008 levels.[4]

Per pupil spending in Bridgeport public schools is low compared with that in most towns in Connecticut. In 2013–2014, $13,883 was spent per pupil, compared, for example, with $20,747 in wealthy Greenwich, 30 miles down I-95, a difference that exists despite federal and state funding formulas meant to work toward equalizing local school budgets.[5] That difference represents over $110,000 for the administration, resourcing, and teaching of each class of 24 students. For Catholic schools, data comparisons are more difficult, but a 2009 survey showed per pupil spending in Catholic schools at $7,743 compared with a public school average that year of $8,402 (a national figure that varies substantially along with regional cost of living and district socioeconomics).[6]

And although Ann Marie is one of the best of the best–she has been New England Catholic School Teacher of the Year and recipient of the national Catholic School Tim Russert Making a Difference Award–various forces including pay tend to put the most accomplished teachers to work teaching wealthier children.[7] About half of Ann Marie's students and, in most public schools of the city, over 90% of students qualify for free and reduced lunch– one index of the reality that Bridgeport is the poorest city in the richest state in America.

Much of Bridgeport's extreme poverty is recent, coming with the deindustrialization of a city that boomed first with whaling and shipbuilding in the 19th century and then with the armaments industry during the world wars. By 1930, there were 500 factories in the city producing a diversity of goods including sewing machines, cars, and corsets. The offshore flight of manufacturing capital from the nation in the 1970s and the relocation of corporations to wealthier towns were followed by the flight to the suburbs of the earlier generations of White immigrants who had made Bridgeport home. African American families and immigrants replaced them. More inequality and crime in the 1980s brought further population loss.

The public schools suffered with the sharp erosion of the city's tax base, official corruption, and the declaration of bankruptcy in 1991. In recent years, amid reports of failing schools and budget crises, the city's contentious board of education was taken over by the state; that takeover was then deemed illegal by the state supreme court and the elected board restored. Intense public debate surrounds efforts to add to the number of charter schools, which proponents argue would increase parental choice. Bridgeport's stark segregation, however, means that parents sending their children to any schools within the city have no choice but to send them to an underfunded school.

At the same time, the city's Catholic schools have undergone quieter changes. Several schools were recently consolidated in light of declining enrollments resulting from shifting demographics and rising tuition (the latter to cover rising labor costs associated with lay versus religious teachers). This made for tough adjustments as teachers like Ann Marie lost some of their familiar collegial support networks.

The morning of our visit, some students were practicing for the poetry recitation. Others were at work reading through research for their project, collected in folders with Ann Marie's neatly lettered, detailed tips on note taking, sourcing, Modern Language Association bibliographic style, the location of local libraries, and timelines for tasks en route to the final product. Then everyone gathered to discuss *To Kill a Mockingbird.*

Within minutes, the back-and-forth was at an excited pace: When Charley pronounced Boo Radley "crazy," others agreed, but Ann Marie guided them to a more nuanced view with a series of questions. What kinds and degrees of "crazy" might Boo be characterized with? Should he have been institutionalized? Does this character remind you of anyone else in the book who feels like they are on the inside looking out? Thoughtful participation was rewarded with enthusiasm and praise ("Gimme five, Angel, that's a good connection")—and more questions.

A midcourse correction came when Jordan and Tanesa began criticizing the character for his immaturity. "Boo doesn't know how to be a grownup because he has been treated like a kid for so long," Ann Marie explained, modeling empathy. She prodded, "Would you laugh at a 6-year-old?" This provoked Jordan's realization that Boo "is like a child stuck in an old man's body."

"I really like that," she said, writing it on the board. After nearly everyone had participated, it was time to move on. They were set to work in teams illustrating the setting based on the text's description.

Before long, the students had to pack up their heavy stacks of books and move to their next class, and another English class moved in. Here the discussion was squared even more directly on society and ethics. Someone raised a passage that had intrigued her: "It says if a boy cries he is a real man." Ann Marie asked, "Do you believe that?" We are trying, she told them, to understand the social and political setting, trying to understand how society expected people to behave then, to understand what it expects now.

She then drew attention to what the "foot-washing Baptist" appearing in the text might symbolize. "People who exaggerate the Bible," offered one girl. "People who think you have to be perfect," said another. And next, where the public school teacher wouldn't go: the explicit integration of religion and literature. "Does Jesus want us to be perfect?" No, many answered, heads shaking. In the end, we saw another lively discussion and broad participation, a second group of 8th-graders who mostly seemed to have read, engaged with, and enjoyed their assigned book. As the class filed out toward the poetry assembly, they passed Ann Marie's message on a bulletin board: "You are the author of your own life story."

* * *

At one time, today's teachers sat, as children, watching teachers teach. Some decided then what they would eventually like to do. So it was for Ann Marie: "Since I was a little girl, in the summertime I would have classes on the back porch, and all the neighborhood kids would come, and we would color and do letters and write stories." Her role models were the Ursuline sisters at her Catholic school in a Cleveland neighborhood not terribly different, she said, from where her students live. Though she is White, this shared urban upbringing and her sense of "universal personhood in Christ" connect her to her students, even as a muted national debate continues about the predominance of White women in America's increasingly non-White classrooms.

As a teen, Ann Marie attended an all-girls Catholic high school where she made good friends of some teachers. While she considered other careers—nursing and journalism—she realized that her squeamishness (even food scraps in the kitchen drain turned her stomach) and her less-than-aggressive personality made teaching a better match for her.

Her parents were the children of Italian immigrants, her mother a telephone operator and then a call center worker. Her father was a wholesale food distributor whose college years were brought to a halt by World War II. Ann Marie was first in her family to get a degree. After moving with her husband to Bridgeport, she started at Cathedral, which several generations of her husband's family had attended. Two years later, she left to have her three children, returning when the oldest entered kindergarten. Choosing to teach in the Catholic system meant making less than her public school peers (on average, $43,500 versus $57,000 per year) and "a struggle" to pay for her own children's college education.[8] This struggle intensified when her husband, a bank auditor, was laid off in a restructuring, though they ultimately put their children through Notre Dame, Georgia Tech, and Fairfield University. It also explains why Ann Marie never earned a master's degree. Although she told us this with explicit embarrassment, a debate exists over how much and what kind of advanced education teachers need to be effective.[9]

Her first assignment on her return was an 8th-grade class of 33 students, 25 of them boys. This was an unwanted group that the other teachers called "the Sweathogs," an allusion to the motley but endearing crew at the time appearing on television's *Welcome Back, Kotter*. One day early in the year, she found a *National Geographic* on her desk, opened to a page displaying one of the naked women that helped make the magazine popular among readers with zero interest in geography. Her students sat quietly with hands folded on their desks, "expecting me, I think, to rail into them. I just said, 'Oh, wow, I'm so glad you appreciate the beauty of the human body.' And it so diffused them."

She had passed their test. And they had passed hers. "It was then that I said, 'I really like this grade.' Because you can reason with them, you can talk to them, you can discuss, you really could treat them as adults and they would rise to it." Her pleasures in teaching continue to come from these moments when—despite gulfs of age and race and even religious tradition—there is this connection. "It's the light that goes on in their eyes when they get something. And they're so excited and eager to prove to you that they learned it and they're growing."

When we interviewed Ann Marie in her warm, family-photo-filled Bridgeport apartment on a chilly May Saturday, she told us, "This time of year it's also exciting to see how far they've come from September." Like many veteran teachers, Ann Marie often doesn't need formal assessments to tell her when she needs to reteach material: "Some of them are nodding and you can see from their eyes that they're getting it, but others are like, 'What the heck is she talking about?' So you have to talk in a different way, or give a different example until you see their light go on."

Asked to sum up why she teaches, she said, "You want to be able to challenge them. It's the growth. . . . [And] *I* want to grow. I want to be alive. I want to constantly learn something. Where else could you do that?"

Catholic schools educated nearly 2 million students this year, about 4% of the nation's K–12 total. While some teachers there may be on the wait for better-paying slots to open up in the public schools, these schools become a lifelong home for many who see their jobs as an integral part of their faith. Ann Marie shares some of the same goals and challenges of public school teachers: preparing for life children with a wide range of ability, personality, and home and community challenges.

Just because Catholic schools are private institutions, she isn't spared cumbersome bureaucratic requirements for documentation, intrusive standardized testing ("It seems just when you're getting them back to a routine, then you have to stop and do the testing and then you get back in. It's very herky-jerky"), top-down directives about the minutest details of pedagogy, and less-than-ideal class sizes (while one of her cohorts includes 24 students, the other has 27, a number much larger than the national average for Catholic schools).[10]

And Ann Marie, like many teachers in all sorts of schools, is frustrated by the public perception of her job as, on the one hand, easy, and, on the other, an on-demand "babysitting service." Those attitudes are exhibited by a few parents who unapologetically pick up their children from school an hour and a half late. "People think you're a teacher, you get out at 2 o'clock, you have vacations free. [But they] don't know. It's 24/7. I have phone calls to parents to make this weekend, papers to correct, plans to do, it's all-consuming." She is right, of course: Full-time teachers report an average week over 50 hours long, working in the classroom, mentoring, and grading, and they spend several summer weeks in continuing education and in preparation for the new academic year.[11]

One disturbing sign of these attitudes is how few Cathedral students talk about becoming a teacher. And, she says, she can't blame them: "There are no television shows, there are no reality shows or movies about education unless they are making fun of it, like *School of Rock*. I don't think they have a background for respecting it that much." This is sometimes true even in a school where many immigrant parents are committed wholeheartedly to their children's education and may also be working on their own GED or college credits. Yet, says Ann Marie, "for the most part I don't think people really think about teaching as a career."

These similarities with teachers in secular settings aside, Ann Marie experiences a school day that is distinct. We saw how it begins at 7:05 in a staff meeting with a morning prayer ("Mary, Mother of God, blessed are thou and the fruit of thy womb Jesus") led by Mr. DiPalma, the principal. He asked if anyone had an "intention," a focus for his or her collective prayers. After receiving and praying on a few, he proceeded to administrative matters, including the procedure for student retention as the year end approached.

Faith structured the announcements after students arrived in their classrooms as well, with prayers of thanksgiving and prayers for "our poets, and the God-given talent we all have to write poetry." The crucifix over the chalkboard and a 2-foot cerulean-blue-robed statue of the Virgin Mary atop the supply cabinet aside, this is not the Catholic school of the past. Where once virtually every Cathedral student came from a family of practicing Catholics, Ann Marie has found that today just a third to a half are Catholic (although the national figure is a much higher 84%).[12] Ann Marie, who teaches religion classes as well as English and history, has shifted from focusing on specific Roman Catholic doctrine to more ecumenical messages. Although most of the student body identify as Christian, many do not attend religious services, and her job, she feels, is also to encourage more active religiosity: "I say to them, you're at the age now where you are responsible for your spirituality. You can ask mom and dad to take you to the mall, or to go to somebody's house for a party. You can certainly ask them to drop you off at church. They don't have to go with you, but now it's in your hands."

While the students worked on their *To Kill a Mockingbird* illustrations, we had the benefit of a tour of the building from two official student ambassadors. Tanesa told us she had wanted to be an obstetrician since seeing a delivery on *The Learning Channel*; Donzel hoped to be a lawyer or a paleontologist, inspired by the Power Rangers' paleontologist-hero and by the protagonist of the video game *Phoenix Wright*, an attorney whose cases "he always took based on trust."

The pair proudly showed us the combination gym/auditorium; the 30-unit computer lab ("we just finished a unit on robots"); the separate Spanish, art, and music rooms; and the Catapult Learning Room ("for kids who need extra help"). They also pointed out the values messages posted everywhere on the walls. A chart of aspirational Gospel values listed "Trustworthiness," "Fairness," "Responsibility," "Respect," "Citizenship," and "Caring." Donzel explained that they learn about a "Gospel value of the month"—this one's was "Faith"—in religion class with Mrs. Donnelly. Another bulletin board identified May as the month of Mary, "our Mother and our Model." Another encouraged students to be "Prompt, Productive, Polite, Prepared." Around the corner, we reached another wall covered with a string of hand-lettered stars radiating out from a banner titled "Random Acts of Kindness," the aim of which was "making the school a more Christ-like environment." Each star celebrated a student's good deed. The plan, Tanesa explained, was to "get them to snake around the whole school."

Our tour guides alerted us to how strongly the students have tied their identity to Cathedral: They continually suggested that they were people who respect each other, who are generous with each other and the community, who have high expectations for themselves, and who have the best teachers in the city. And here, Donzel said, they "can talk about God."

In the end, we asked Ann Marie what she thought was necessary for being a good Catholic schoolteacher. Was being a good teacher who is also Catholic and willing to teach religion all that it took?

"No, no," she said. "The kids have to see that you struggle with your faith." She explained that almost a decade earlier, her brother-in-law and his wife had been killed in a high-profile robbery. "And it was a death penalty [case], and there were people who were against it and people who were for it. And I felt so bad for my niece and nephew who were wonderful, who really rose above it, but I struggled as a Catholic. You don't believe in the death penalty, or you think the death penalty is wrong, but let me tell you, I was the first to say to the kids, this bothers me. I'm struggling with this. Because I can't forgive this man yet." Not long afterward, a nephew was killed in a car driven by a drunk driver, and then her husband succumbed to cancer. She struggled openly again with her students, not about *what* her faith taught her to think but *how* it helped her frame her questions and how she used its resources to make her way through.

Ann Marie chose teaching because it allows her to have a full, human relationship with many young people, year after year. One especially strong set of friendships came from the class she taught the year she lost her husband. When she returned to school a few weeks after his death, the children, she said, "didn't know what to do. You could see that they were struggling. What do we do? And one student walked over and gave me a hug. And every other one of those students came up, there were 30 of them, and they all said, 'Group hug, group hug!'"

Near the first anniversary of her husband's death, which fell in her birthday month, she got a phone call at home. One of the group huggers was on the line asking if she could come visit. Within minutes 12 students were at the door with balloons, cake, and flowers. They knew the birthday would be a hard one, and they wanted to make it easier. This group now visits each year for pizza and conversation. "I feel like I'm having one of those old French salons because they talk about everything."

Ann Marie's clearly not done teaching yet. Like most teachers of literature, she understands that reading and writing connect us to the human family. Her posted sign "Reading Thought of the Week" said as much and more: "We need to know we are not alone."

Questions for Discussion

- How similar are the experiences of teachers in private schools, religious or otherwise, to those of teachers in public schools? How do they differ?
- What kinds of character education, faith education, or teaching about social justice are appropriate in different school settings?
- How should teachers navigate teaching their values when their classrooms are diverse in that regard?
- How much and what kinds of fundraising and resourcing from the community should teachers take on?
- What can be done to equalize educational opportunity in a nation of increasing inequality of wealth and income?

Suggestions for Further Reading

Adams, M., Bell, L. A., and Griffin, P., eds. *Teaching for Diversity and Social Justice*. 2nd edition (Routledge, 2007).

Bauch, P. A., ed. *Catholic Schools and the Public Interest: Past, Present, and Future Directions* (Information Age, 2013).

Cho, Rev. Young Kwan. "The Relationship Between the Catholic Teacher's Faith and Commitment in the Catholic High School." *Journal of Catholic Education,* 15, no. 2 (2012): 117–139.

Duncan, G. J., and Murnane, R. J. *Restoring Opportunity: The Crisis of Inequality and the Challenge for American Education* (Harvard Education Press, 2014).

Scheopner, A. J. "Irreconcilable Differences: Teacher Attrition in Public and Catholic Schools." *Educational Research Review,* 5, no. 3 (2010): 261–277.

Lisa Myrick

chapter 3

Doing Woman's Work
The Gendered Science of Teacher Pay

(Gilbert, South Carolina)

Lisa Myrick had to toughen up early. She was in the 9th grade when the First Gulf War broke out, and her father, a Vietnam vet and X-ray technician, was called up out of the U.S. Army Reserves, shipped off to Kuwait, and then sent on to Saudi Arabia. Soon after, her mother, a nurse and also in the Reserves, was sent to Fort Campbell, Kentucky. For a while, Lisa and her siblings stayed behind in South Carolina, living with friends so they could keep going to school.

But she didn't have to tough it out alone. In an act of kindness that changed the arc of Lisa's life, a teacher reached out. Ms. Trautwein called and asked if she could come over—she'd made dinner for Lisa and the family. It struck Lisa even at the time that this was above and beyond, a gesture from which her teacher had "nothing to gain." After several months, their mother was able to relocate the family to Fort Campbell. There also, teachers kept a special eye out for these children who'd been uprooted from their home. Before long, the war ended, and so did Lisa's parents' marriage. There was a separation and a divorce. Soon, their father had a new wife. Once again, during the upheavals, teachers filled a void. These "very touching and memorable" acts would help lead Lisa into a profession for which she had developed a profound respect.

When we spoke on the phone to arrange to visit her in South Carolina, Lisa was brought to tears recalling Ms. Trautwein, but we discovered that Mama Myrick, as her students at Gilbert High School call her, is a tough cookie who doesn't crumble easily. In person, the high school science teacher is a tall, blond, no-nonsense fast talker, by southern standards, whose enthusiasm for her subject rivals that of television's science evangelists Bill Nye or Neil deGrasse Tyson.

Lisa isn't afraid, for example, to teach climate change to public school children in a Deep South state where there's no such thing as tenure, which can protect teachers from punishment for venturing into politicized academic territory. As she spent a recent summer preparing to teach AP environmental science, she vowed that the conversation would not revolve around whether or not the climate was changing. Instead, it "would be why is it changing and what are we going to do to stop it. I just kind of dug my heels in and did not even allow for, 'Well, my daddy says that this is just all bull.' I totally prepared myself for it, and I came out swinging." The unit went well. The extra work–gathering "tons" of empirical evidence to present, finding a text pitched at her students' reading level–paid off. She crafted a unit to reach her particular student population without sacrificing what she knows is good teaching.

Introducing nonscientific ideas in a science classroom does both teachers and students a grave disservice, Lisa believes. She was proud that a state senator's push to shoehorn creationism into the science curriculum had been held off–though she was frustrated that his effort was ongoing and the fight wasn't over yet. The proposal on the table when we met Lisa would insert language into the South Carolina science standards that would encourage "teaching the controversy," following a legislative strategy of anti-evolution forces. Teaching the controversy casts doubt on evolutionary theory and allows the introduction of intelligent design and other nonscientific theories into classroom study. Not just in the South but across the country, teachers must contend with the politicization of science. Some succumb. In one survey of American public school biology teachers, only 28% self-identified as advocates of evolutionary biology and among the 60% who reported advocating neither evolution nor creationism are many who "want to avoid controversy."[1]

Because not all science teachers are as knowledgeable or confident as Lisa, the National Center for Science Education provides resources to help educators effectively teach topics such as climate change and evolution that are academically complex and politically controversial. Key is helping teachers understand the arguments of climate change deniers and evolution doubters and then arming them with clear, empirical rebuttals. Efforts such as this may go only so far, however, in helping teachers resist the tide in states such as Wyoming, which rejected the Next Generation Science Standards, explicitly citing the negative effect teaching human-made climate change would have on its coal and oil industries.[2]

Lisa doesn't teach Gilbert High's biology class, but she does touch on evolution in AP environmental science, and in chemistry, she told us, "when we talk about where elements come from and supernovas, the fact is–and I say this–we're all stardust. What we're made of comes from the stars. Knock on wood: I know one day I'll get an email or a phone call." Thus far, she hasn't fielded complaints, a silence that speaks to the trust afforded her and the school by the community, however conservative.

Maybe it would be different if she weren't South Carolina born and raised. Twice a graduate of University of South Carolina, where she received her bachelor's in biology and her master's in teaching, Lisa has moved out of state a few times but has always come back. For the past 6 years, she has been living in Gilbert (population: 497) in a 19th-century farmhouse with her husband, Brad, an entrepreneur, and their three children. Although she pins herself as an ideological "oddball" for the region, she's no stranger in town. Out and about, she can't help but run into parents, who ask how their children are doing in class. "I have no anonymity. None. I'm Mrs. Myrick wherever I go."

It's less than a half-hour drive from the town hall in Gilbert to the state-house in Columbia and only minutes to the city of Lexington's strip of chain restaurants and big-box retail stores. Still, the tiny town feels a world away from these relative megalopolises and can seem suspended in time. While the main thoroughfares are paved, plenty of roads remain rutted dirt tire-poppers; family farms have somehow held back the tide of exurban development overtaking nearby towns; and the biggest event all year is July's Peach Festival, which boasts the Annual Peachy Tractor and Antique Farm Equipment Show and where, in 2013, the Lexington County Peach Queen happened to be the daughter of the 1982 winner.

During the school year, Gilbert High parents and teachers are more likely to see each other at a football game than at Curriculum Night. And on the Indians' expansive athletic fields and in the crowded bleachers on any given weekend, it might seem as though school life hasn't changed much over recent generations. But inside the school, where Gilbert's students are learning in a very 21st-century way, Lisa Myrick would like to see the community push its children as hard in academics as it does in athletics.

Gilbert High's main building is handsome, and the wing that houses Lisa's classroom is brand new. She teaches in the Center for Sustainable Solutions, opened in the 2012–2013 school year as one of seven Centers for Advanced Studies located at various Lexington County District high schools (other programs focus on agribusiness, public health, and law and global policy). A glass-lined atrium for collaborative work and a videoconference room give it the feel of a well-endowed college campus. Each student in Lisa's large classroom has his or her own iPad, and students take notes from an electronic whiteboard connected to Lisa's desktop and take multiple-choice tests on hand-held "clickers" that instantly tabulate their results and produce an item analysis that allows Lisa to see how they performed on specific questions.

The program offers environmental science, Energy Management Solutions, and physics and macroeconomics classes with a focus on sustainability. State-of the-art lab equipment allows Green Building Solutions classes to learn how renewable energy works and learn how to construct ecofriendly buildings. Students can receive college credit, achieve accreditation in green building practices, and participate in internships.

But Lisa had warned us not to be "fooled by appearances"; we shouldn't assume that the school's shiny facilities reflected its students' home lives. Gilbert, like many American towns, has rich and poor, but most residents are of modest means or just scraping by, working in retail, construction, or agriculture.[3] Yet because its schools belong to Lexington School District One, which is a larger district, and one willing to fund major facilities construction despite a national trend of austerity, Gilbert has access to resources that some small towns don't have, providing hope that more of its children will prosper.

On the day of our visit, Lisa apologized that we wouldn't see much "teaching"–an unprecedented ice storm the previous week had meant missed school days, and a unit-end test in her honors chemistry class couldn't be delayed. But a lot can get done during the center's 90-minute periods, and Lisa stole as much time from assessing as she could for learning. As students finished their tests, they could start on textbook reading they'd been assigned for homework, and when all were done, they would share their work on an interdisciplinary research project they'd completed.

After the last test takers returned their clickers, Lisa announced the class average: 93%. The crowd was pleased, except for one self-flagellating boy, who insisted he'd bombed: "If it hadn't been for me, the class probably would've gotten 100." Scanning the results, Lisa responded that no one had scored below an 80. "Say you swear," the boy demanded, brightening out of his disbelief. Lisa announced she would post their individual results in the electronic gradebook before day's end. Another boy pumped his fist in anticipation.

Lisa paused to review an outline for the upcoming chemical bonds unit, which she had emailed them. ("We're supposed to post this all on our websites, but email is quicker," she insisted, admitting to a microact of resistance to micromanagement.) Students could see all assignments and assessments for the next 2 weeks. There would be no surprises, no excuses for them not to complete their work–or for Lisa not to complete hers. Still, there is some flexibility in the chemistry curriculum, allowing her to take advantage of current events. Weeks earlier, she had come across an article in a science education journal about the chemistry of the Olympic torch.

With the Olympic Games in Sochi, Russia, under way, the students had read the article and completed a related worksheet. Now, she asked them to recall the scientific information they had gleaned from the piece. Then she called on class members to share their homework: collages illustrating research on the geography, history, and politics of past Olympic Games produced using an iPad graphics app.

After this, there was time for a mini-lesson on the combustion of propane, an Olympic torch fuel. As they took notes, a peppy redheaded student mentioned they'd be more likely to remember it if they wrote it down, likely parroting a Mama Myrick refrain. "By the end of the semester," Lisa reassured them, "this formula will pop into your heads and you'll be able to balance these equations. Chemistry is another language, and my job is to get you thinking in that language."

After she graduated, Lisa worked for 2 years before marrying Brad, moving with him to Augusta, Georgia, and having their children. When her kids were old enough, she returned to teaching. One thing that Lisa had loved about the job was the independence, but when she returned to teaching in 2008, No Child Left Behind and the standards movement had reshaped the educational landscape. Gone was the significant autonomy she had enjoyed as a new teacher.

"My friends in education kept trying to tell me, 'You're not going to believe it when you get back, with the end-of-course testing and the state-mandated testing. You're in for a shock.' And I was."

Her first year back, Lisa taught physical science, then a course that South Carolina students had to pass to receive their diplomas. The course's teachers were all required to give, each on the same day, seven unit tests over the semester, tests drafted by the district. The results were instantly transmitted to central office administrators, who either rewrote poorly constructed questions or instructed teachers to reteach material. All was in service of preparing students for the end-of-course test. "And we did prepare them," Lisa told us. "We had high passage rates." (Ironically, after spending much time and money developing the course and its assessments, the state suddenly stopped requiring the physical science class. Now students must pass biology to graduate.)

The new focus on data also struck her as occasionally absurd and frustrating. For example, racially speaking, Gilbert is an anomaly in the state: while 4 in 10 rural South Carolinians are African American, Gilbert is overwhelmingly White. So when Lisa got a stern "talking-to" after district data highlighted a dramatic gap in the achievement between Whites and Blacks in her class—that is, a dramatic gap between the test scores of the one Black student and the rest of the students—it was hard not to wonder what rabbit hole she'd fallen down.

And Lisa initially bristled at being told what tests to give. Eventually, she accepted that a genuine effort was being made to help more students pass required courses. She also sees how new teachers can benefit from a set curriculum and linked assessments. A bit "rusty" from having been out of the classroom, she found that not having to develop her own units or tests made her first year back easier. Yet teaching had changed, and Lisa wasn't sure she was going to like the new order. That's because what might be uplifting to a new or struggling teacher can stifle an experienced or proficient one. Since Lisa was asked to join the center, her course load has consisted mostly of honors and AP classes; she no longer has to teach one of the lock-step basic science courses. This gives her greater control over how to deliver the curriculum and assess learning, which means she's always trying new methods. In turn, her teaching has improved and her enthusiasm has grown. It's this kind of "engaged autonomy" that strong teachers say is essential to their development.[4] (Unfortunately, this pattern, of higher-level classes affording greater autonomy to their teachers, likely reinforces the nationwide reality that higher-achieving students tend to have better teachers than do struggling students.)[5]

From its unveiling, the Common Core has been polarizing. Yet a vast swath of America's teachers responded initially, as did Lisa, with optimism. When we visited, only math and English standards had been established, but Gilbert's science teachers were being expected to teach to them. Where she sees an opportunity to address the standards and achieve her objectives, Lisa does so: The worksheet accompanying the Olympic torch reading she assigned her chemistry students is a good example. It included strategies to build skills in reading for information suggested by the standards. She was surprised by the frenzied reaction to the Core that had built among some teachers, parents, and the public. Her response: "People, calm down! The kids just need to know how to read better! Just calm down; it will be okay." She wondered if those adamantly opposed to the Core had "even read the standards."

Her response to the district's somewhat dogmatic requirements for the use of technology has been similarly pragmatic. Spending on education technology in the United States has been exploding despite cuts in education budgets at the local, state, and federal levels; it is expected to nearly double from 2013 levels to reach $60 billion by 2018.[6] (For perspective, the entire current federal education budget is $141 billion.) The Lexington district has been working to keep pace. Considerable sums have gone toward constructing wired buildings, providing students with tablets, and supplying staff with educational hardware and software; in turn, Gilbert teachers have been directed to use technology to take attendance, grade, and communicate and to educate—by integrating it into every lesson.

Like her colleagues, Lisa has spent innumerable hours searching for—and teaching herself—apps she can use meaningfully, an undertaking that is "intimidating and overwhelming." Before long, she stopped trying to force technology into every aspect of her teaching. The reality is that some days, paper and pencil and whiteboard and marker remain the best teaching tools even though they're not glamorous. Lisa recalls learning from teachers who taught the same way every day, who approached lessons with a by-golly-I'm-going-to-teach-you-how-to-do-this attitude. "Some of the best teachers I had as a student had a piece of chalk and they were ready to go."

If this science teacher believes that technology can improve instruction only so far, it may be because she believes that teaching is no science but an art. "Either you have the heart of the teacher and the desire to be a teacher or you don't. It's an art to look into the eyes of 30 kids and know by the way they're looking back to you that they understand."

In AP environmental science, there was a touch of fear in the eyes of some when Lisa announced they would each soon be making a formal presentation to parents and the public at an open house. The project required students to choose and independently research a topic (this they were excited about), produce an annotated bibliography (this elicited an audible "Yuck!"), and prepare a 6- to 8-minute formal presentation (this seemed far off, provoking unsolicited advice on time management).

Once she'd reviewed a rubric detailing how they would be evaluated and previewed the project's components, Lisa had students pick topics under the heading of sustainable solutions to environmental problems. The classroom came alive; students tapped on tablets, swapped ideas, showed Lisa articles on wildlife preservation, microbeads in cosmetics, the California water crisis. Approached with potential topics, Lisa pushed for greater specificity and urgency. When one boy asked to research plastics in the oceans, she questioned, "What about it?" To a girl who'd asked the meaning of a word: "Look it up!" To another boy: "Start now. Get off Flappy Birds and look to see what's there."

Real-world, relevant, interdisciplinary, research-based, multimedia: This was project-based learning. The class was on it, yucky parts and all.

* * *

Interviewed in the center's breezy courtyard, Lisa, the rational scientist, became self-conscious sharing her emotions about teaching. "Sometimes I feel like a buffoon," she said. "I get a little embarrassed of my own enthusiasms for it." After describing how tough the first years of teaching are, after listing the additional burdens that have been tossed on teacher's loads, and after acknowledging that new tasks and stresses are likely ahead, she concluded, "Eventually, it's fun. I'll say it: It is fun." And then, as though confessing to a crime, she added, "I like it. I like my job."

We asked why. "Just to be a part of shining a light on something that a kid had no idea about, to me, is invaluable. To hear when kids say, 'Chemistry is fun; chemistry is not that hard.' That's great! Seeing a kid appreciate learning is just invaluable. You can't put a price tag on it, which is probably why I will never leave." Echoing Ann Marie in Bridgeport, she relayed the joys of staying in touch with former students. She explained how one, on active military duty in Afghanistan, had posted a video of a televised debate about evolution on her Facebook page, asking, "Mrs. Myrick, did you watch this? It was amazing." He wanted to talk about it, so they did, via videochat.

Most of the center's students go on to college, almost exclusively in state: to Clemson, the University of South Carolina, or Erskine or another Christian college. The day of our visit, Lisa learned that a student she admiringly described as "deeply interested in the natural world" had gained acceptance into Clemson's competitive pre-veterinary program.

"In what other job do you get that?" she asked. "They stay in touch, let you know when they're getting married. I feel very maternal, and I love these kids. I want to see them grow up. There's certain special ones: I'll think, she's going to have a cool life, and I can't wait to hear how it turns out."

If there's one thing that Lisa Myrick wishes—and it's not a small thing—it's that teaching paid higher salaries and was held in higher esteem. Even her parents didn't want her to teach. Without directly stating she could be more successful doing something else, they made their feelings clear. Her college advisor was more explicit, actively discouraging her by arguing that scientific research needed more women. This only cemented her decision. Her parents' reaction, however, still pains her. "They never really smiled upon this career choice of mine," she said wryly. When she was named Teacher of the Year, she invited her parents to the ceremony, but neither came; when her police officer brother, however, was promoted to station chief, the family traveled from all corners to celebrate his achievement.

Whether or not parents encourage their children to become teachers is one measure of the profession's social status. Job status motivates teachers and facilitates more effective collaboration with parents and students. Critically, it also affects the profession's ability to recruit strong candidates. A recent study showed that teaching is held in lower esteem in the United States than in, among other countries, China, South Korea, and Singapore in the East and the Netherlands, Turkey, and Greece in the West.[7] And teachers enjoy significantly lower occupational prestige than workers in most other traditional professions, including professors, doctors, and lawyers; teachers rate similarly to those in other feminized professions such as nurses, librarians, and social workers.[8]

In the United States, income and status are closely linked. Yet America's secondary school teachers are paid 72¢ on the dollar earned by all working college graduates, compared with 90¢ on the dollar for teachers in other OECD (Organisation for Economic Co-operation and Development) countries.[9] Critics argue, of course, for raising pay overall to address this disparity. Some reformers have proposed merit pay as a way to lure, reward, and retain candidates; in recent years, performance-based pay has been a key element of reform in a number of states. Research into its effects remains limited, though there is some suggestion it could help retain high-ability teachers.[10]

Lisa was observed by us on the same day that one of the nation's most well-known and controversial reformers, former Washington, DC schools chief Michelle Rhee, was in Columbia, South Carolina's capital. She was testifying at a hearing in favor of House Bill 4419, a proposed piece of teacher evaluation legislation that would institute merit pay (albeit without any associated funding) in South Carolina.[11] While her chemistry students concentrated on their test, Lisa circled to us and, containing a smile, whispered the news that H4419 had failed to make it out of subcommittee.

Lisa would seem to be exactly the kind of teacher to respond to the idea of merit pay: She is motivated and talented and could easily obtain a better-paying job. So why wasn't she in favor of the measure?

The bill required that 50% of her teacher evaluation would be "based on evidence of growth in student achievement," wording Lisa found vague and problematic, especially as she teaches a subject not covered by state standardized tests. What then would provide "evidence"? What was meant by "growth"? How would it be measured? These were just a few of her questions. "Any teacher knows that scores on a test may vary greatly from year to year," she told us, "although she may have taught the material using the same practices. What is different is who walks through those doors in August and what their prior experiences have been. Did they travel to the Caribbean this summer or did they get bounced between foster homes?" She concluded, "Performance-based pay is scary. I get nervous enough when I am waiting on my AP scores without the threat of a pay cut or the promise of a bonus." Here is a teacher, highly valued by her district, who doesn't need the hope of earning a little more money to work hard and smart and who surely doesn't need the anxiety of earning a little less.

A recent survey of the research demonstrated that merit pay plans—which vary widely in type—have no clear impact on student achievement.[12] And the most rigorous study to date, conducted by Vanderbilt University, showed that offering bonuses to Nashville teachers to increase student scores on standardized tests had no effect.[13] The available research also reveals no clear patterns in the components of merit pay plans that might make them more or less effective in improving outcomes for teachers or students.[14] The appeal of these plans has been based largely on political and fiscal considerations: The Obama administration's Race to the Top lists merit pay among the "innovations" its grants seek to promote. Sadly, merit pay may remain a thrust of reform efforts as long as the notion persists that our nation's educational problems derive from a stable of bad teachers who need both carrot and whip to giddyup.

Lisa Myrick was, after 8 years of teaching, making $42,000 a year, compared with a median salary for intermediate-level clinical research scientists in her area of over $70,000.[15] And while she insisted that no one should consider education as a career if student well-being is not the top concern, the pay in fields using her degree is rarely far from the back of Lisa's mind. She has long understood that her husband's income enables her to teach; she didn't need the rude wake-up call she had received the year before when Brad suffered a heart attack. Although his recovery was swift, she didn't need those terrible hours in the hospital to know that without him, she would not be able to afford to teach. There would be three children to send through college on her own. As we saw in the Bridgeport case, it is a sad fact that teachers struggle to provide their children with their same level of education.

Lisa believes that year-round school could help elevate teachers in the public's eyes (while doing wonders for students, she adds). "From the outside it looks like maybe the greatest job in the world. You get weekends off. You get 2 weeks at Christmas and summer off." But, she said, "over snow break, as I call it, I work on school work every single day. Over Christmas break, school work every day. Weekends, Sunday afternoons . . . I don't think people realize that, and I don't know that you could raise awareness of that to the public. They'd just think you're whining." Many teachers must work for a paycheck during the summer to make ends meet. Those more financially fortunate, like Lisa, engage in other kinds of work, often without compensation, on behalf of schools and students; Lisa attends AP institutes, chaperones overseas biodiversity tours, and writes curriculum for new classes. But the stigma of "summer off" sticks.

As she ruminated on why the profession receives less respect than it deserves, Lisa identified a likely reason: "There are a lot of women in this profession. I think it stems from that." It's women's pay for women's work. The silver lining, and it's a big one, is that unless and until merit pay spreads, it is a rare profession in which women are paid equally to men for doing the same job.

After our interview, as evening's light dropped behind the tree line, we followed Lisa home down Gilbert's winding roads, interrupted Brad and the couple's two sons shooting hoops in the driveway, and headed with them to Lexington for dinner. At the Mellow Mushroom, we ordered pizzas and settled in for a night out with the Myricks. While the adults chatted, the boys played games on their smartphones and the youngest, a girl, drew quietly. And we felt as we often did when with teachers in their homes, schools, or communities: grateful to be spending time with education's true experts.

Questions for Discussion

- How can teachers hold on to their content expertise and the values of their discipline when many—the sciences, social sciences, and literature among them—have become politicized? How can they negotiate differences between personal, pedagogical, and community beliefs?
- Can meaningful education reforms be consistently undertaken without stripping teachers of autonomy?
- How much can technology improve teaching and learning? What level of knowledge and use is realistic to expect from educators, given the pace of technological change?
- Does the predominance of women in the profession help explain teacher pay and status? What other cultural factors are at play?
- What would constitute fair pay for teachers?

Suggestions for Further Reading

Berkman, M., and Plutzer, E. *Evolution, Creationism, and the Battle to Control America's Classrooms* (Cambridge University Press, 2010).

Eggers, D., Moulthrop, D., and Clements Calegari, N. *Teachers Have It Easy: The Big Sacrifices and Small Salaries of America's Teachers* (The New Press, 2005).

Figlio, D. N. "Teacher Salaries and Teacher Quality." *Economics Letters,* 55, no. 2 (1997): 267–271.

Greaves, T. W., Hayes, J., Wilson, L., Gielniak, M., and Peterson, R.. *The Technology Factor: Nine Keys to Student Achievement and Cost-Effectiveness* (MDR, 2010).

Ingersoll, R. M. *Who Controls Teachers' Work? Power and Accountability in America's Schools* (Harvard University Press, 2006).

Robert Lewis

chapter 4

Alternative Paths to Teaching and Exceptional Students in an Age of Standardization

(Colorado Springs, Colorado)

The middle school was administering a new state social studies test. The state department of education and the test maker, Pearson, were trying to work out bugs in the online test with this pilot, but as the assistant principal announced to the students at laptops in the library media center, "We're testing the system, but the test itself is tied to you: It *counts*." The look on the faces in front of him must have prompted him to reiterate the point: "What you and others across the country are testing is *accessing* the test, but the test itself *is tied to you.* Do not exit the test without the help of the adults in the room because if we have to get you back into the test, we have to call someone in New Jersey."

A social studies teacher acting as a proctor attempted to chime in on a more positive note. "You are very lucky, because–" she began, interrupted by a student's grumbled complaint that they had just taken another test days earlier. The boy rose, seeming ready to bolt from his seat. He was reprimanded by the assistant principal. Another boy asked haltingly, "Does this affect us . . . our high school . . . ?" His anxious voice trailed off.

The assistant principal tried to explain why their "data" was being collected, warning it would follow them in their files: "That's how classes will be determined, whether you go to the next grade level, whether you graduate, so don't think it doesn't matter." Another administrator elaborated that guidance counselors would look at their test results to answer questions such as "Does Isaiah get an elective or does he get a remedial class?" The assistant principal reminded them that their attitudes also mattered because the minutes it took them to finish the test would be recorded.

Then the proctor recited Pearson's script of instructions, painstakingly reading through sample questions. She called a librarian over to help with the headphones that students with individual education plans for learning disabilities were using to take the test with supplementary audio. Finally, it was time. "Ready? Begin."

Were it not for the model Atlas rocket standing in the center of the library, this scene could have taken place anywhere across America, where testing occurs in a steady drip all year but intensifies as spring testing season opens. That morning, though, we were at Jack Swigert Aerospace Academy in Colorado Springs, named after an Apollo 13 astronaut. Once a traditional public school rated as failing under the federal No Child Left Behind initiative, it was closed and reopened as a charter school run by the Edison Schools chain. That charter, in turn, closed, and in 2009, with the help of the Space Foundation, a nonprofit promoting the space industry and space education, the school reopened as a STEM (science, technology, engineering, and mathematics) magnet. Controversially, such whiplash closings and reopenings have been happening elsewhere, across the country, in concert with urban education reform efforts.

We'd been invited to Swigert by Robert Lewis, whose title there is learning support teacher. Robert has a caseload of 22 7th-graders identified as needing special educational services. Another teacher works with the high-needs students mostly on life skills; Robert's students tend to have specific learning disabilities that he considers mild and include several children on the autism spectrum. He coteaches mainstream classes, including social studies, with regular education teachers, teaches math to small classes of students on his caseload, and tutors students who are struggling or need extra support.

The day we visited, the school was on a special schedule, and Robert had been assigned to proctor the state test. Because enough adults were on hand in the library, though, he was able to take us on a building tour.

Three years earlier, Robert Lewis had taken his first teaching job at Swigert. While most new teachers enter the profession on graduation from college, Robert was 51 years old, having spent most of his adult life in the military. Although he'd grown up in Colorado Springs, for 3 decades he'd been in constant motion, stationed at various bases overseas and stateside, working for the air force in a transportation management position requiring frequent travel. He met and married his wife in England, where they had two children. While stationed in South Korea, he volunteered at an orphanage school and found it fulfilling, but it was a presentation by representatives of the defense department program Troops to Teachers that led him to consider teaching as a second career. The program helped him get started on coursework toward certification before he left the military. Even so, when he first left the air force, Robert worked briefly as a mortgage broker. Within months he realized that what he wanted to do with the rest of his life had less to do with money and more to do with people. He wanted to teach, and he wanted to teach the children who needed him most.

Robert has a personal history with disability that equipped him with the empathy, skill, and will to work with students some educators find too challenging. His brother had been disabled by polio, and his son, at age 2½, had been diagnosed with high-functioning autism. These experiences instilled in him the intense belief that all children can learn and that all deserve an education enabling them to fulfill their unique potential.

Many of Robert's students work with multiple challenges. Some live in poverty; some learn with English as a second language. Many, Robert told us, are transient, so they are new to the school, their home, and the city, and they may be new to another school and city before too long. Like middle schoolers everywhere, they contend with the social–emotional turmoil of early adolescence, but in their neighborhoods, as they grapple with identity formation, they face the added danger of being lured into gangs. Overlaid on these challenges are their specific learning disabilities, which can make it more difficult to learn in traditional ways. We met some of them as testing ended and they entered Robert's room for Fundamentals of Math. At the bell, four students had arrived; a fifth came in with a pass, having been held after his last class.

"For something good or something bad?" Robert asked, examining the pass.

"Something good."

"Liar," the others teased.

Although the 7th-grade group was small, it was lively. Ethan, thin and vibrating, chomped furiously on a wad of gum. Desirae, the sole girl, whose earrings spelled "Foxy," had a generous laugh. Finally, Alex arrived, and then there were six, with enough energy and banter between them for a class twice the size.

Robert handed each a math sheet they would compete to finish first, a friendly daily competition that focuses them quickly. "Ready? Begin!" The room plunged into silence; it was quiet enough to hear Robert tapping on his keyboard and the soft smack of Ethan's gum. As they finished, they ran to give the sheet to Robert, who happily announced, "You all beat the time!"

"I'm not giving you anything too stressful today because some of you had testing," he announced, splitting them into two groups and handing each a deck of cards to play a math game. This gave him a chance to pull students individually to practice, with flash cards, their multiplication tables, which he needed to make sure each had down pat as the class moved into multiplying and dividing integers.

He started with motion machine Ethan. Legs, arms, shoulders, hands–some part of the boy was in movement at all times. Ethan quickly ran through the multiples of seven correctly, pumping his fist as Robert shuffled the cards. (Meanwhile, Alonzo and Jeremy shuffled their deck to play another round, singing, "Everyday, I'm shufflin'," a pun on rap lyrics.) Robert gave Ethan a high five, and they moved on to multiples of eight.

After getting a couple wrong in a row, Ethan became discouraged: "I missed a lot."

"You're doing fine. Trust me," Robert reassured him.

Ethan put his head in his hand. He started throwing out wild guesses.

"If the one we just did is 56, it must be bigger."

"Sixty-four!"

One of the groups had turned from playing the math game to doing magic tricks.

"You are supposed to be playing Twenty-Five," Robert reminded them.

Then it was Owen's turn to join Robert, but he had something other than multiplication on his mind.

"My brother got in a fight with my mother this morning."

"Not a good morning, huh? Your mom doing okay?"

"Yes, he was asking for $18, and then he got greedy about it."

"Did it make it hard for you to test this morning?"

"Yes."

"Do you want to talk to anyone about it?"

"No, I'm fine."

The unprompted interchange was brief. Owen's recounting seemed to understate the tumult with which his day had started. But Robert's lap was a safe place to drop that burden, and Owen seemed lighter for it.

Volume rose among the card players. Robert said, "That test made you crazy today. You guys are not yourself today. Okay, let me work with Owen, guys? Don't make him nervous."

*   *   *

With No Child Left Behind, states were pushed to include more special education students in their standardizing testing regimens; with this came a complex effort to provide students with disabilities with test accommodations that could allow them greater opportunity to demonstrate their knowledge. Accommodations might include extended time, oral presentation, or an alternative setting for test-taking. Yet even with these, issues of the fairness and validity in testing special-needs students, especially given the diversity of disability, remain.[1]

Robert has strong views about how standardization and an overreliance on testing do a disservice to children with special needs. Inspired by the British advocate for arts education Sir Ken Robinson, Robert believes every child is different and that ignoring this difference means terrific waste. With a cookie-cutter approach to education, "a lot of talent is lost along the way." While there's been an attempt to add an *A* for "the arts" to STEM, converting it to STEAM,[2] Robert still sees art and music being sidelined as reading and math are pushed hard. There are students, he said, for whom the core subjects will never be their forte, no matter how good their instruction. This doesn't mean they can't learn to read well or to do math well. Yet, in Robert's view, "we aren't taking advantage of some of their talents" and this boils down to the reality that "we aren't educating some of our kids."

For all children, he believes, "it's fine to learn, but it's even more important to think. I think that's the ultimate goal. Change doesn't come from things that you already know. Change comes from things that you don't know. Particularly since No Child Left Behind, we want them to know. That's not teaching kids how to think, you're teaching them things that you want them to know. We really need to rethink what education is all about. For me, it is accessing your individual potential. No matter what field it is. I don't think we need to be so narrow-minded as to say every kid has to pass this state exam in order to be educated."

On the one hand, the resources at Swigert allow for the kind of hands-on learning experiences that help many special-needs children to thrive and that can develop problem-solving skills for all students.[3] Title I monies and grants, including those from the Space Foundation, provide Swigert with a healthy budget. Walking around the school, it was easy to see where many of these dollars were going. Robert took us out to the science wing, which houses a Mars Rover Lab where students build and test run robots on simulated Mars terrain. Filling the hallway, seven enormous cardboard boxes containing professional flight simulators awaited installation in another lab. In a broadcasting classroom complete with a green screen, kids learn how to record and edit video and audio on Macs. Here, students produce daily announcements and an episodic mystery.

Pressure, however, is intense to lift the school's standardized test scores, which lends itself to test prep and rote learning. It is on these scores, not the craft with which the best robots are constructed or the creativity with which the televised mysteries are written, that the school's status as a failing school rests. In response to test scores the prior year that were up "a little but not very much," Robert explained, a block schedule had been instituted to provide extended class periods of language arts and math every day, 90 minutes each devoted to this "core content." The time had to come from somewhere, of course, so electives including art, music, and physical education are fit into 90-minute classes every *other* day.

In fact, the school's test scores remain stubbornly low despite the many changes the school has undergone. In 2013, only 25% of Swigert 7th-graders scored at or above proficient on Colorado math tests, compared with 48% for the district and 55% for the state; in reading, 43% scored at or above proficient, compared with 66% in the district and 68% in the state.[4] This can be discouraging for both students and teachers. Not all instructors are as patient with the students, their behavior, and their progress as is Robert. Teacher turnover at Swigert remains high, with, Robert believed, more than 20 new teachers hired this year, nearly half the faculty.

As in the Gilbert case, spending on technology was highly visible. Speaking broadly about where money is being directed in education and where it is not, Robert pointed out that every room in his school has a Smartboard, every 6th-grader has a netbook and every 7th- and 8th-grader a laptop, but at the same time some other needs may be neglected. Desks and chairs looked battered ("I think, from the '70s," he speculated) and about ready to pop their screws. And though Robert didn't bring it up, Swigert teachers and their district colleagues had been working under salary freezes for several years running and had taken forced, unpaid furlough days because of districtwide budget cuts. Of course, this meant schools were closed those days.

In 7th-grade math, Robert asked Alex—red cheeked and sporting an incipient mustache—to show us a software program called Vmath. Alex carried his laptop over, plunked himself down, and patiently demonstrated the program. Modeled after social network games such as Farmville, Vmath delivers lessons and tests that students can complete to earn points and "coins" they can use to play games against other children. When students reach certain levels, they can decorate their avatars and obtain new ones. We asked Alex if he liked the game. "Yeah," he replied with the brevity of a tween asked a fairly dumb question.

Meanwhile, Robert worked with Desirae on her "sevens," fending off her claims that it was too difficult. "It's too hard?" he teased. "But then next week, you'll tell me eights are too easy! Right?" She grinned. Robert had explained that many of his 7th-graders understand math concepts but have problems memorizing. The flash cards help build their memory, he told us, and they get quick individual feedback, quick individual successes. His high fives seemed to provide more motivation than any exotic new avatar.

During the next period, which included the lunch rotation, only one student, Joaquin, was in attendance in Robert's Fundamentals of Math class. Robert asked if he had homework for another class, since they couldn't move forward with a formal lesson. Joaquin didn't think he did, but Robert said, "Let's check." Together, they looked over his assignments in various classes and made a study plan. Part of this plan involved logging onto the Achieve 3000 differentiated reading program, which generates nonfiction articles at the students' level, based on tests they take. The articles are followed by comprehension questions and writing assignments. Joaquin began reading one right away, which maybe didn't just *happen* to be one about an astronaut. It's very astronautical at Swigert.

Robert could give this individual attention to Joaquin in part because of the absence that day of others. In fact, absenteeism is high in urban schools across the country, and it is rising, along with the poverty rate. It is also high among students in special education classes.[5]

Robert makes himself available during the lunch period to give students a chance to get extra help or "just hang out." No one dropped by right away, so he headed out and pulled a boy named Blake out of a class that was working on ratios; Blake needed some remedial work with multiplication and integers before he could tackle that new unit.

Back in the room, as he worked with Blake, Robert spied a boy lingering near the door and waved him in. This was, perhaps, a student he'd mentioned to us earlier who he'd been worried was "shutting down."

The boy moved somewhat listlessly into the room.

"Having a good day, Justin?"

"No."

"You want to do this"–indicating the math work he was doing with Blake–"or just hang out?"

"Just want to sit."

Justin wrote a pass to the cafeteria, had Robert sign it, disappeared, and returned with a tray, to eat his lunch in this quiet place.

At several points in the day, we watched Robert teach and reteach concepts to a child using one method, then another. In his view, if a child isn't learning material, the teacher hasn't found the right way to teach it to that child yet. "People need to take more time to understand them," he said. "I hear people say, 'Kids don't want to learn.' You can't force a kid to learn. Kids will let you know that they want to learn. That's something I don't think people understand. You don't pour the information into their heads–they have to process it." It is up to the teachers to figure out how each of those students learns best, he argued. "I never think that they can't do it. I always think, okay, well, we just have to get to it another way. There's a thousand ways to climb a mountain."

He is also adamant about providing extra services to children without stigmatizing them. "I don't talk about special education." His self-contained classes are called Fundamentals classes. And in those classes that he coteaches, such as social studies, he tries "to integrate into the classrooms as much as we can." To any child in that room, he's just another teacher. They all ask him for help, "regardless of whether they're on my caseload or not. I think that that's important. Then the kids that are on my caseload don't feel singled out or feel like, well, I don't want to be around Mr. Lewis because then everyone will know I'm 'special.'"

Robert can seem like an idealist. Then again, that very week he had taken his autistic son, then living at home and attending community college, to visit a 4-year college in Oklahoma he was planning to transfer to. Robert hasn't just seen what a child with the odds against them can do; he's already helped one beat those odds.

* * *

On our building tour, we bumped into a master teacher who travels between district schools observing newer teachers like Robert and giving them feedback on their methods. She explained that this would be her last year providing this service to her colleagues, as the grant that funded what was called the Teacher Advancement Program (TAP) was about to expire. Research on the effectiveness of TAP has shown mixed effects on student achievement and teacher retention.[6] Yet these kinds of coaching programs may be especially helpful to teachers who have pursued alternative routes to certification.

As do roughly half of Troops to Teachers recruits,[7] Robert went on to complete a master's degree in education. But he did that while working at Swigert in a tutoring position and before being hired as a full-time certified special education teacher. Depending on the state, however, teachers who take nontraditional routes to the classroom may spend years in front of students without much or any traditional teacher education.[8]

Since the inception of alternative routes to certification–New Jersey was the first state to craft one in 1983–their number has exploded. Roughly one-third of all teacher preparation programs in the country are alternative programs.[9] In 2011, one out of six new teachers entered the profession via one.[10]

This growth has come despite limited research to date on how successful these programs are in recruiting, training, and retaining effective teachers.[11] Proponents argue that by making teacher preparation less costly and time-consuming, alternative routes bring into the profession more bright, highly educated career changers and more graduates of highly selective colleges. They point to data showing that alternative routes deliver more men and more people of color to the neediest urban and rural schools.[12]

Critics counter that traditional programs require meaningful hours of supervised clinical training and additional hours of student teaching, both of which novices need before they are handed responsibility for a classroom. Perhaps the most controversial alternative route program is Teach for America (TFA), which recruits graduates of elite universities into a 2-year teaching commitment. TFA has been criticized for sending its young, mostly White recruits into low-income schools with just 5 weeks of training and, since so many do not stay on after 2 years, has also been blamed for exacerbating already high rates of teacher attrition in these schools.[13] Most critics might be happy to see recruiting and job placement organizations such as Troops to Teachers continue to attract male, ethnically diverse, and older people into the profession but steer them toward traditional certification programs.

Both Robert and his students benefit from the credibility that his age and experience provide. For some young teachers, for example, parent meetings can be anxiety provoking, and for new special education teachers they can be especially so, since meetings around individual education plans (IEPs) are a legal matter and can be emotional, even contentious. "I rarely ever stress over IEP meetings," Robert told us. "I enjoy talking with the parents." He has no hesitation discussing with parents their children's disabilities, a delicate subject. Whether it's his age, his military service, his community roots, his own experience as a parent of a special-needs child, or the composure and quiet confidence all this affords him, parents grant Robert the respect he deserves. And when parents and teachers can collaborate in identifying how best to help a child, that child wins.

There's also something to be said for Robert being a highly accomplished Black man who can act as a role model for Swigert's children of color, who represent three-quarters of the student population.[14] In some states, just as the percentage of students of color in the public schools is growing, the percentage of non-White teachers is declining. Yet the research has shown that students of color are academically advantaged when assigned teachers of their own race or ethnicity—or even just go to school in a district in which these teachers are well represented.[15]

Robert thinks about his students even when he doesn't think he's thinking about them. One day, he told us, he'd been puzzling how to find a new way to teach a prealgebra concept that was stumping some of them. "That particular night, I woke up with an idea, thinking, 'Oh, that will work!'" It involved a color-coded mat and buttons that would help visual learners understand the effect of multiplying positive and negative numbers. "I had to actually make it first, and it's not pretty, but it works; that's all I care about. When I ran to school in the morning, it took me about 20 minutes to throw it together, and I tried it out, and it was like, 'Wow, that's it.'"

As the day progressed, Robert sought out more students for extra help. Ponytailed Socorro, dressed in black, was shy and a bit uneasy; she seemed like she might prefer to hide in a large class than be singled out for such one-on-one attention. Robert pulled her from her math class to work on ratios, which she'd been struggling with. The class was moving ahead into the unit. Robert began with her by looking up and reviewing the dictionary definition. "All it is," he explained, "is a division problem. You can write it these four different ways."

The tension eased from Socorro's body. Her unfinished practice packet on ratios sat to the side as Robert clarified that what mattered was not in that packet but in her mind. What mattered was not how quickly that packet got done but that it did. With our visit coming to a close, we understood that the most important thing that Robert gives his students is time. He's giving them more than simply individual attention from a caring adult; he's actually *giving them time.* In Robert's classroom, students get a rewind so they can catch up—to where they can be, maybe where they should be, maybe where many of their classmates are. The subject matter hasn't passed them by. They don't need to give up.

"For students with specific learning disabilities," he told us, "where it might take you or me 5 or 10 trials to understand a concept, for them it might take a 100 or 150, so you have to really reinforce, reinforce, reinforce, reinforce, and they learn." That takes time. And it might not happen on the same schedule as the state's standardized tests.

Robert showed Socorro ratios using manipulatives but also demonstrated on paper. Only then did he move to the packet—to a word problem she'd missed about the ratio of juice to water that various imaginary people had in their glasses. The worksheet asked, "How did you get your answer?" "We divided," she said, looking for reassurance in Robert's eyes. He asked her to write down the full answer ("We divided what?") then went for a high five. "Are you ready for the next one?"

As they kept working, the bell rang. But she didn't have to rush out. Robert would write Socorro a pass for her next class so that she could finish up. They completed one more ratio problem.

"Wow, you're a star!"

Questions for Discussion

- What is gained and lost when an emphasis is increasingly placed on tested subjects?
- Should schools be labeled as "failing"? Should standardized tests be used as the key criteria in judging a school's success?
- What are the benefits and risks to the profession brought by the proliferation of alternate routes to certification?
- Can special-needs students be fairly assessed using standardized tests?
- How important is it for students to be educated by those of the same race, gender, or cultural background? If they don't share these with their students, what can teachers do to mitigate any issues created by differences?
- How can new teachers best be supported? How effective are teacher evaluation programs such as TAP?

Suggestions for Further Reading

Darling-Hammond, L., and Lieberman, A. eds. *Teacher Education Around the World: Changing Policies and Practice* (Routledge, 2012).

Dudley-Marling, C., and Baker, D. "The Effects of Market-Based School Reforms on Students with Disabilities." *Disability Studies Quarterly,* 32, no. 2 (2002). http://dsq-sds.org/article/view/3187/3072

Jobs for the Future. "The STEM Workforce Challenge: The Role of the Public Workforce System in a National Solution for a Competitive Science, Technology, Engineering, and Mathematics (STEM) Workforce" (U.S. Department of Labor, April 2007).

Koretz, D. *Measuring Up: What Educational Testing Really Tells Us* (Harvard University Press, 2008).

Overton, T. *Assessing Learners with Special Needs: An Applied Approach* (Pearson, 2011).

Heather Frantz

chapter 5

When Parents Become Teachers
Opting Out to School at Home

(Perrysburg, Ohio)

Offering nationally known speakers, an exhibition hall bursting with vendors, and hundreds of workshops over 3 days in Cincinnati's huge convention center, the MIDWEST Homeschool Convention is as big as any regional education conference. But when Heather Frantz began attending it 6 years ago, the event was small enough to be held at a church.

Having just started home schooling her two older daughters, she was anxious and uncertain, fearing failure. The convention reassured her. She was not a weirdo or a lunatic for choosing this path; nor were the other attendees apparent weirdoes or lunatics. There were experts she could meet and good tools with which she could equip herself. Although she had chosen to be home alone teaching her children, she was not really alone.

Heather's confidence has grown in tandem with the home schooling movement, itself a substantial flank of the school choice movement. An estimated 2 million American children are now educated at home, more than double the number in 1999.[1] Home schooling advocates estimate a higher total, one that approaches the charter school population. Yet while charter school goals, successes, and failures receive generous national press coverage, allowing some insight into what teaching and learning are like there, the work of home schooling parents remains something of a mystery to educators and the public.

We felt privileged, then, to be invited to spend time with the Frantzes, who educate their four children at home in a Toledo suburb. It is one thing to ask to visit a classroom; schoolteachers are accustomed to observers. It is another thing to ask to plop down on the couch in someone's family room, stare at her children, and start hammering away on a laptop.

Arriving at the family's traditional colonial in the midst of a neat middle-class neighborhood, we were set at immediate ease. They came by twos to greet us at the front door. The eager faces of kindergarten-aged Emme and Isabelle appeared in the window as we hurried up the walk through whipping rain, and when we rang the bell, two hyperkinetic white puffball puppies named Gizmo and Maya ran in circles, we imagined, to welcome us onto the ark.

Morning in the Frantz household was notably calm, a marked contrast to the predawn chaos of homes where parents and kids simultaneously rush toward the exit. Activity ramped up slowly but surely. The two "Littles," as the family calls Emme and Isabelle, outfitted in matching hot-pink capris, tees, and tiny wire-rimmed glasses, were put to work at the granite-topped kitchen island practicing handwriting in identical workbooks, and in the adjacent dining room 13-year-old Madelyn settled in to start on a list of tasks for the day. Soon, Anna, the eldest at 17, padded downstairs fresh from the shower, dressed in sweatpants and T-shirt. Slipping in next to Madelyn at the dining-room table, she opened a math textbook.

When Anna was in the 4th grade, Heather presented the case to her husband, Ty, that she should homeschool the children. Madelyn was then in kindergarten, and the Frantzes had just entered the long process of adopting the two youngest from China.

The argument was this: Volunteering at Anna's private Christian school, Heather had seen too much busywork, time wasted transitioning between activities, and assigned reading that wasn't an appropriate challenge. Students' ideas about who was good at what (and who wasn't) were already being set in cement, and Anna came home from school joyful only when the gifted teacher had been in and wished "every day was like the gifted day." Their inquisitive child was losing interest in learning. Nor did it seem like things were headed in the right direction. Madelyn's kindergarten experience was more intense than Anna's had been, as new expectations for the lower grades were stressing out teachers and students.

By contrast, witnessing the growth of the children of several home schooling friends convinced Heather that they were getting a better education. She could give that to their children, too. Home schooling provided great flexibility in how, what, when, and where learning occurred, her children could be given individualized attention, and she could address their learning styles in a way that a teacher with a classroom of students could not. Finally, she could spend more time with her children, watch them reach milestones instead of experiencing "resentment over the amount of time that traditional school was taking from our lives." Strengthening family bonds was a driving force, especially as the Frantzes anticipated incorporating two new members who would be arriving from 7,000 miles away.

The Frantzes' motives are typical of those of America's home schooling parents in that they are complex and various and evolve along the way.[2] Research shows push factors dominate: In one survey, 91% of parents said they "are concerned about the school environment, such as safety, drugs, or negative peer pressure" and 74% cited "dissatisfaction with academic instruction at other schools."[3] Plenty cite the pull factors of "a desire to provide religious instruction" (77%) and "a desire to provide moral instruction" (64%). The stereotype of the American homeschooler as a conservative Christian has some empirical support here, though there are homeschoolers of every religious and political stripe. Liberals can be found among those citing the various reasons to homeschool, but especially among the 44% with "a desire to provide a nontraditional approach to [their] child's education."

As Heather chatted with us, the Littles moved on from handwriting practice, at Emme's urging, to a math coloring book. Heather paused to help each one in turn. Exuberant, chatty Emme finished quickly, eager for the next activity; the more reserved Isabelle took her time.

Isabelle was adopted first, coming to Ohio at 14 months; Emme came later at 3½. There were some early physical challenges with Isabelle, whose developmental delays were, like those of many children raised in Chinese institutions, significant. Heather explained, though, that "given the chance, she caught up in record time. It was like watching child development in fast-forward. She crawled within 2 weeks and walked within 6." Emme was adopted from an orphanage housing 500 children, 20 to a bedroom. "A lot of kids," Emme told us, adding, as though saying the name would help her hold on to the memory of her bunkmate, "Chi-wah was next to me." Her records showed that Emme was developmentally delayed, but the Frantzes didn't know exactly what that meant. At more than 3 years old, she wasn't yet talking, but Heather pointed out that she was now the most voluble of her four children: "Clearly she could talk!" Gross motor skills were an issue, but Emme developed quickly. Friends questioned the Frantzes' ability to teach her English, but Heather was unworried. She'd taught three other children the language, she'd told them.

After the girls had a quick snack, Heather presented two cookie sheets and poured a thin layer of rice on each, making a cheap manipulative for learning and practicing numbers and letters.

"Can you draw me the number 10 with your finger in the rice? How about 11?"

When they got to 12, both girls put the two first; Heather reminded them that teens start with the one.

"Thirteen . . . 14 . . . 15 . . ."

"Mom, I like this!" Emme enthused, enjoying the tactile sensation.

"Sixteen."

"How do I write 16?" Emme asked.

As they worked their way up the numbers, Emme would ask Heather how to write it, and Heather would ask her to think about it. At 20, a new challenge.

"How do I write 20? Tell me, please?" Emme asked, hands under her chin and head cocked.

"She's putting on a show for the audience today," Anna, relocating from the dining room with a chemistry book, noted.

"You wrote it in your math book already today!" Heather reminded Emme.

Finally, she drew a two, then a zero. Looking up, she flashed a grin.

Heather had explained that Emme was still overcoming some learned helplessness she had acquired in the orphanage. But she'd had enough victories to feel an increasing sense of agency. Reading, for example, was difficult, but she'd had a recent breakthrough, reading a whole page.

Next, Emme and Isabelle worked with Heather on a geography lesson using wipe-off maps. The dining-room door quietly shut, and from behind it came the muted sound of Madelyn practicing the piano. Then the rain stopped, and Heather sent the younger girls outside to play. Anna, closing her chemistry book, asked her, "Can I just say what I have to do for the rest of the day? The two SAT rewrites, poem analysis, working on quizzing; I did the math, I finished science." With the teens increasingly independent, Heather can spend more of the day with the little ones. Anna had largely overcome problems she'd had with time management; Madelyn, who for years liked to "do school" on Heather's lap, was working more on her own. Still, all needed some one-on-one attention, and this meant juggling. Madelyn's least favorite subject is reading, so Heather continues to work with her closely on that. When Heather and Anna retired to the family room to work on a recitation project, the Littles arrived to show off paper birds they had constructed, Madelyn popped in on them chewing a sandwich, and Anna complained, "It is only the 5 minutes that I want to do something that all three of them are in the room."

The "official school day" wound up around 3:00. By then, Heather had helped Madelyn answer reading questions she was stuck on and had cuddled up with the Littles on the couch to read from *The First Animal Encyclopedia*, which became not just a science but also a math lesson (as they read about the albatross, Heather sent Emme to get a tape measure so they could visualize its 15-foot wingspan); Anna had analyzed an Edgar Allen Poe poem, using the Internet to educate herself on the sonnet form, and had read a portion of *Crime and Punishment*; and Heather had served lunch and then given formal reading lessons to Isabelle and Emme in turn, each while the other built a fort of pillows and blankets nearby.

* * *

Homeschoolers do not work without oversight from the states. In Ohio, either students can take a standardized test at year's end to prove what they learned or parents can submit a portfolio of students' work for review.[4] But no one—no department head, no principal, no superintendent, no government official—is telling homeschoolers *how* they must teach this material. Still, certain methods have become widespread among home schooling parents. Classical education methods based on the Greco-Roman trivium, which brings children through the stages of grammar, rhetoric, and logic, was popularized among homeschoolers by the work of evangelical theologian

Douglas Wilson.[5] Heather periodically sends Emme and Isabelle to a weekly classical education class that involves "lots of rote memory." Although "it's like being fed with a fire hose," it is Heather's job to do something with all that knowledge, delivered based on a "timeline from Creation to the present day," that the girls take home with them.

Heather also finds appeal in the approach of Victorian-era British educator Charlotte Mason. Like classical education, the Mason approach emphasizes the liberal arts, but is child centered and focuses more on concepts than on facts. Heather described it as "the loving, nurturing approach." The formality and rigor of classical education fits Heather more comfortably, yet she appreciates how aspects of the Mason approach, such as encouraging children to spend time in nature, exploring and journaling, push her to work against type. "I want them to be thinkers, and I want them to be curious."

Homeschoolers' use of pedagogies and materials that originated centuries ago results in part from a deep cultural and religious conservatism: The texts in the traditional Western canon were overwhelmingly written from within the structures of a Christian ideology. Contemporary texts lean toward subjects and attitudes that Christian conservatives find immoral, offensive, or inappropriate. Nonetheless, Heather was self-conscious about some of the educational time travel she engages in. What would we think of her using one of the McGuffey Readers, first published in the 1830s?

Heather contended that American schools are in a continual process of "reinventing the wheel," with increasing and needless complexity, while home schooling parents can avoid wasting time on fads. "I want them to be educated, in ways I wasn't educated, I guess, in ways that kind of meld things together more for them. Help them make connections." Allowing her children to explore their interests and study them in an interdisciplinary way is part of this, but so is blending "their faith with history and not keep[ing] those things completely separate."

This intertwining was visible all day. Emme and Isabelle's handwriting workbooks used words and images from scripture. Anna's textbook was titled *Exploring Creation with Chemistry*. Madelyn was studying *The Odyssey* in an abridged version in *The Children's Homer*, which excises scenes deemed too risqué such as Odysseus's visit to the Underworld and his 7-year dalliance with the sexy nymph Calypso. While religious public school teachers can struggle to reconcile their beliefs with the curricula they are assigned to teach, religious home schooling parents can select from a growing body of texts such as these, explicitly crafted to deliver their values. No worries about having to "teach the controversy" about evolution as discussed in the Gilbert chapter; there is no controversy.

The insecurities Heather felt in the early days of home schooling were revived when time neared for Anna to register for college admissions testing. Homeschoolers can largely avoid standardized testing, but the SAT and ACT are a game, Heather said, they must play. How would Anna do on the SAT? Well enough to get into a good college, succeed there? Feeling as though they might be stumbling in the dark, the Frantzes hired a tutor to work with Anna to get her ready to take her first national standardized test. Then the family visited Grove City College (with the motto "Authentically Christian. Decidedly Conservative") in Pennsylvania, where Anna sat in on classes. Anna's own anxieties were quelled once she realized that the discussions were not over her head; the mode of inquiry was familiar.

As the home schooling movement has grown, a central concern has been whether parents can be relied on to fully prepare their children for college or career. Home schooling in the elementary grades is one thing, critics argue, but high school? How can someone without wall-to-wall diplomas manage to effectively teach physics, calculus, computer programming, chemistry, world history, literature, Spanish? It's a reasonable concern, particularly when many parents struggle to help with some homework sent home from traditional schools even in the early grades.

Homeschoolers exploit various means to try to overcome their individual content area deficits. They enroll their teens in selected courses at local colleges, community colleges, or high schools when those children's readiness for a subject eclipses their knowledge; distance learning is increasingly an option; and then there are local cooperatives of home schooling parents, each bringing different strengths, who can teach each other's children. The Frantzes belong to one of these cooperatives, to which we tagged along the next day.

These co-ops, too, partly help answer critics who contend that home schooled children can suffer from isolation and a lack of community socialization. Ty often says he thinks their children suffer from *too much* socialization when you consider the sum total, including church activities; the family's community service, which has them volunteering weekly in a poor Toledo neighborhood; and the relationships they've developed through the co-op. It seems that the type rather than the amount of socialization is what differs for home schooled children: more time spent with adults than peers, more socializing with, not away from, the family, and more interaction with people with shared values and experiences. Heather explained, "For some families, absolutely, they want to shelter their kids; they don't want them to be exposed to things. I'm not really worried about that. I'm fine with my kids being exposed to things, [but] I guess I like the ability to expose them to those things in *my* time." She wants to control when, how, and where her children have certain experiences. Some teens learn about drugs and addiction from peers and in health class, for example; Heather's would learn about them under parental supervision as the family worked alongside recovering addicts at the soup kitchen.

Every Tuesday, Heather and the girls pile into the family minivan and drive to the Christian Fellowship Church in an adjacent town. The teens spend much of each Monday getting ready for classes at the co-op, which were already under way when we arrived in the morning. Every nook and cranny of the building was in use. Upstairs, 12- to 15-year-olds, including Madelyn, met for writing and a history, theology, and literature class called Omnibus; Anna and older teens were downstairs for chemistry; the Littles joined the youngest for music. Later, the chorus rehearsed in the nave to an audience of empty pews. In the basement, children rejoined their families at round tables for lunch and for breaks between classes.

Co-op classes are taught by mothers of co-op students; these include some former schoolteachers. Demographically, the parents reflect the majority of America's homeschoolers: White, well educated, and middle-class.[6] In this way, they mirror the nation's schoolteachers. And just as teaching is female dominated, home schooling "is largely a movement of women."[7] Mothers in home schooling families are overwhelmingly the parents who direct their children's education; many are women who can afford to stay at home and invest in home schooling usually because they are married to men who work in the professions or are gainfully self-employed. Heather's husband, Ty, is CFO at a midsized building materials company. The socialization provided by co-ops like these then may fail to provide home schooled children with exposure to people of other ethnicities, income groups, or ideologies. (At the same time, unfortunately, as we witnessed in Bridgeport and Colorado Springs, while the country is becoming more diverse, many American children attend schools that are socioeconomically if not racially segregated.)

Heather teaches the Omnibus course at the co-op alongside Mrs. Schmitz. The two provide a nice balance: Heather's soft, firm manner is calming, while her coteacher is feisty and energetic. Heather opened the class with prayers as latecomers slid in on what was a slushy morning. Then Mrs. Schmitz took over for a lesson on revising. After brainstorming strategies for improving paragraphs, the class worked in groups on a paragraph on King Solomon by varying sentence openings. A group of eager boys added "a –ly beginning" to one sentence and worked with amusing effect to use vivid verbs: "Frantically, two arguing prostitutes ran toward Solomon—no, *dashed* toward Solomon."

Heather then led a discussion of *The Odyssey*, using the higher-order questions from among a list that students had answered for homework. In one instance she asked, "What are temptations in the modern world that people get lost in, like Odysseus gets lost at Calypso's?" A number of students offered suggestions: video games, drugs, books, comic books, television shows, Legos, fame. "What are the consequences?" Carpal tunnel from computer overuse, social isolation, not spending time outdoors, letting life revolve around the temptation. Her follow-up question: "Why are we here?" Their answers: to give praise to God, to help others get out of that web. Heather elaborated, "To know God and help others know him. So when we get lost in these entertainments that God has granted us, we need to wake up."

What followed was a lively discussion of other key scenes, and a reading from the unabridged text of Odysseus's trip to the Underworld. Heather used this opportunity to mention, "We've talked a lot about why we read the classics and why we read pagan literature, and we do because the language is beautiful. And I hope you can see that from reading the original." Still, the literature, characters, conflicts, and themes are always tied back to scripture.

"Proverb 7," Heather taught, "is the argument against Calypso, the smooth-talking woman: 'He followed her like an ox led to slaughter.' Anyone of any gender can be smooth talking and lead us away into temptation. Let's look at Luke 4, verse 1. Grab your Bibles."

Abby read the story of Jesus's temptation after 40 days in the desert. The students agreed with Heather that they could relate to his temptation here ("even though he is God"), and they concurred that it was "absurd" that Satan offered Jesus power.

"It's like I take something from you and offer it back to you," Sam pointed out.

"You'd think he'd be better at tempting people, but these are stupid," Ben said, scoffing at Satan's three vain attempts.

*   *   *

Like schoolteachers, home schooling parents can feel stereotyped and misunderstood. Although it matters less to her these days, Heather thinks home schooling parents are generally viewed as "strange" and "fringy," reactionaries making "a political statement" by taking their children out of the schools.

Also, like schoolteachers, they can perceive that their work is undervalued. Katie was a mom of six we met at the co-op whose appearance defied stereotype: Her curly dark hair threaded with silver, she wore a trendy orange puffer vest, purple sweater, and jeans and had a diamond stud in her nose. She shared with us a call she had received the day before from a parent asking if Katie could take another child at home that day—her response was to laugh out loud. One misconception, Heather said, of home schooling moms is that they are "home all day with nothing to do" and thus can be called upon to babysit or take on extra social or church responsibilities.

Heather articulated great respect for teachers, of whom there are several in her family. While she feels equipped to homeschool, she explained, "I don't think of myself from a professional standpoint at all as a teacher. I think of myself as a mom who happens to educate her kids at home." She made a clear distinction between the professional skills and education needed to manage a classroom and to attain deep content knowledge and the requirements of the work that she is engaged in. "My techniques or approaches are from here and there, but I don't have—that's not my background. Managing a classroom, developing curriculum, I have none of that. Yes, there are moments when I specifically sit down and teach my children something that I know that they don't. But a lot of the time we learn things together. And we're kind of on a journey together." Home schooling and schooling were distinct activities in Heather's eyes, one personal, the other professional. This seemed to allow her to privilege home schooling for her family without denigrating traditional schooling for others, to honor her work without dishonoring the work of teachers in the schools. The question still lingers about the effect that home schooling parents' lack of formal professional training and certification (which they share with teachers in some independent schools, especially religious ones) has on the education that their children receive.

While rigorous research to date is thin, on average homeschoolers appear to be preparing their children well on the journey to college and adulthood. Studies have found that children educated at home perform as well or better than children educated in the schools on standardized tests (although these are not the primary educational goals of most homeschoolers).[8] Of course, home schooling children on average have the advantages of higher household income, better-educated parents, and more intact families compared with the average American child, but the few studies that control for those effects still find some positive outcomes, including in learning styles and habits. Admissions officers' views of homeschoolers are also positive, although data on whether they tend to do similarly or better in college than formally schooled undergraduates are equivocal.[9]

One study by a homeschool advocate found home schooled children overall to have higher self-esteem, confidence, and maturity and that, as adults, they were highly engaged in social and civic activity and report high satisfaction with their education and their lives.[10] On the other hand, one study found positive developmental effects only for teen homeschoolers with religious ties, while those without were at higher risk than their demographically similar public school peers.[11]

Critics of home schooling, conceding that some individual children benefit from it, are concerned about its systemic effect. As with school choice overall, they worry that the exodus from the schools of families that can afford to leave them drains the schools of higher-achieving students and more engaged parents, contributes to increasing racial and socioeconomic segregation, and lowers public support for adequate school funding. Like other segments of the choice movement, home schooling is seen as reducing education to a private, consumer good rather than a public, civic good, a shift that will continue or worsen inequality of outcomes. Other critics are worried about how home schooling contributes more generally to isolationism within American society and the dissolution of the public sphere.[12]

Understandably, successful home schooling can also seem a challenge to the professionalism and competence of teachers, but it need not. The main reasons why home schooling on the whole works has as much to do with factors that make it less than comparable with traditional schooling.

The adult–child ratio at home versus school cannot be ignored. Even when a homeschooler has children of multiple ages to shepherd through multiple subjects, each child is still receiving hours a day of individual attention.

Homeschoolers' success can then become an argument for smaller class sizes, opportunities for regular one-on-one or small-group tutoring, and a greater emphasis not on standardization but on tailored instruction in the schools. Home schooling may also provide evidence that certain types of heightened government intervention in the schools may not improve educational outcomes there: Homeschoolers seem to perform similarly across the nation regardless of how tightly or loosely home schooling is regulated by the state.

And if there is one thing that schoolteachers can learn from the experience of home schooling parents, it may be the value of creating independent learners. Despite the challenges, teachers in the schools can increase opportunities for students to think and act more independently.

Heather Frantz may not think of herself as a teacher, but by the time we left Ohio, we did. Her philosophy of education largely echoed that of other teachers we visited in very different settings, but she stated the moral enterprise most succinctly and distinctly: "To help them understand what it means to be human, and virtuous, and bring value to the world, and to be prepared to do that."

Questions for Discussion

- Do home schooling parents' motivations seem compelling? What might home schooled children be gaining and what might they be missing? Should efforts be made to keep these students in the schools?
- What explains the achievement of homeschoolers on standardized tests and in college admissions reported in the literature to date? What other evidence of these students' educational achievement is needed?
- What are stereotypes of home schooling families? Have your own ideas about home schooling been altered in any way by this chapter?
- What can teachers in traditional schools learn from home schooling parents and vice versa? What teacher training would home schooling parents most benefit from?

Suggestions for Further Reading

Apple, M. "Away with All Teachers: The Cultural Politics of Home Schooling." *International Studies in Sociology of Education,* 10, no. 1 (March 2000): 61–80.

Lebeda, S. "Home schooling: Depriving Children of Social Development?" *Journal of Contemporary Legal Issues,* 16 (2007).

Lois, J. *Home Is Where the School Is: The Logic of Home schooling and the Emotional Labor of Mothering* (NYU Press, 2012).

Lubienski, C., Puckett, T. and Brewer, T. J. "Does Home schooling 'Work'? A Critique of the Empirical Claims and Agenda of Advocacy Organizations." *Peabody Journal of Education*, 88, no. 3 (June 2013): 378–392.

Murphy, J. *Home schooling in America: Capturing and Assessing the Movement* (Corwin, 2012).

Lindsey McClintock

chapter 6

Scripted, Tested, Overworked
Why Too Many Good Teachers Leave

(Litchfield Park, Arizona)

Lindsey McClintock had a sore throat and a stuffy nose. When we arrived in her Litchfield Park, Arizona, classroom on a Thursday afternoon, she'd nonetheless persevered through a long day teaching her passel of 3rd-graders. She welcomed us, adamant we shouldn't postpone our interview. While we worked ourselves into diminutive chairs designed for tinier rears, she placed two cell phones on the table next to her.

The second phone was the result of a little problem she'd run into when she'd started teaching just a couple of years earlier. One afternoon Lindsey had needed to check with a parent to make sure that her child, who was usually picked up, was getting on the right bus home. Using her personal phone opened the floodgates to a string of that parent's calls for the rest of the year, calls at night and calls on weekends asking for homework help. The two phones laid side by side seemed symbolic of the young teacher's attempt to achieve work–life balance.

Lindsey's balance had been off all week. She had been in each day despite being ill, for several reasons a common practice among teachers at her school and across the country. For one, the work of putting together the detailed lesson plans for a substitute can be onerous. More important, the state was in the midst of a substitute teacher shortage. If a substitute cannot be found, a sick teacher's class is split up among the other teachers of that grade. Lindsey didn't want to inflict that on her students or colleagues. Dragging herself through the day often seemed the better option.

It shouldn't be a surprise that in an improving economy, Arizona's typical substitute pay of $85–95 a day or $12.00–13.50 an hour ($11.38 nationally and as low as $8.17 an hour in some other states) fails to motivate qualified college graduates to be on call for an unpredictable day's work.[1] This is a "shortage," though, reported around the country, that allows states and districts to reap cost savings on days when they don't have to pay a substitute but can wring more work from classroom teachers or even bring in volunteers.

It was discouraging then to arrive at Lindsey's school on Friday to find her dealing with exactly the problem she had worked to avoid causing for others. Red nosed but resolute, she quickly found seats to squeeze in the seven extra children who would swell her class because Mrs. Gibson had called in sick.

Once 33 students were crowded around six tables (if all her own students had been in attendance that day, there would have been 38), Lindsey wasted no time. She tucked her long amber hair behind her ears, strode to the whiteboard, and plunged into the morning's math lesson. She drew and labeled a series of shapes on the board, then asked students to copy these in their math journals and find the perimeter of each. Several students raised their hands to explain how they answered the question, and Lindsey detailed these steps on the board.

After the squares and rectangles had been tackled, finally one "tricky one" was left, an L shape.

"What can you tell about this shape?" she asked.

No response but some blinking.

"It looks like it was cut out from a square," she hinted, drawing a dotted line to indicate the square that might have been.

A gasp! One hand shot up, then several. Lindsey waited for more hands to rise over the sea of little heads.

"Now what do I do?"

Eagerly, various children directed her, step-by-step, until the correct perimeter of the "tricky" shape was reached.

Then it was on to solving for area. Again, students dutifully wrote out problems and solutions. After this 30-minute math lesson, Lindsey transitioned swiftly into the daily phonics lesson, using a prepackaged program. The website of the program's publisher describes it this way: "Wilson Fundations for K–3 is a phonological/phonemic awareness, phonics and spelling program for the general education classroom. Fundations is based upon the Wilson Reading System® principles and serves as a prevention program to help reduce reading and spelling failure." It was about as exciting to watch in a classroom as this description is to read–Lindsey pointed to syllables on a bulletin board or paged through flash cards and the students responded by chanting the consonant and vowel sounds in unison.

Lindsey knows the drills by heart; otherwise, she would be required to read aloud the script provided in the *Fundations Teacher's Guide*, which she always keeps handy. "They tell us exactly what to say," she explained. And while Lindsey was reciting the drill, so was every 3rd-grade teacher in the district, saying the same words, on the same day of the week, at the same time of day. This complete lockstep is designed to ensure consistency of instruction but also allows for a certain interchangeability of teachers, one that ensured Mrs. Gibson's students were on the literal same page as Ms. McClintock's.

Although the program seemed stultifying, Lindsey found it effective in teaching the rules of English and in helping students to decode words, spell, and ultimately read and write. The next week the students would take a spelling test, so, after the drill, they took a practice test.

"Reprint . . . crutch . . . calendar . . . collar . . ." After she enunciated each word, students repeated it, then she provided a context sentence, and students spelled it out, applying the rules they'd learned about the sounds of different letters and syllable combinations. When the test was over, students took out colored pencils and went over their answers, noting those they'd missed. Finally, it was time for a break. The 8-year-olds had been seated and toiling for 80 minutes straight. Now they could retrieve snacks from their cubbies.

As the children dug into bags of fruit or Goldfish crackers, Lindsey prepared to read aloud a chapter of the beloved classic she'd been reading them, *Charlotte's Web.*

"Who remembers what was happening last time?"

A boy supplied, "The grandfather was saying Wilbur was going to be made into smoked bacon!"

"And what did Wilbur think?"

A girl quoted, mimicking the pig's horror, "He was like, 'I don't wanna die!'"

Lindsey asked several inference questions and then read the short chapter to a rapt audience. But in less time that it took some to finish their snacks, the chapter was over, and it was time for more math.

The list of things Lindsey has to worry about while delivering a lesson is long. As the second math lesson got under way, she was making sure she called on as many kids as she could ("Who haven't I heard from yet?"); correcting misbehaviors (to a child who called out without raising his hand: "What do we do if we have a question?"); gently dealing with incorrect answers ("No, but this *other* problem could be solved that way"); redirecting off-task behaviors (drawing a distracted girl's eyes back to the board); trying to keep everyone honest (placing a colored pencil in the hand of a child using a regular pencil to correct his work); probing to ensure deep understanding (as students offered answers, asking, "Why is that the answer?"); connecting to prior knowledge ("How is this like what we've been learning?"); noticing when focus and energy start to flag ("After we finish this last problem, it's time for Fun Friday!").

Classroom observers can be tempted to employ the inadequate cliché that a teacher is like a juggler. Teaching, of course, is far more complex, high risk, and exhausting. Over a typical school day, a teacher makes more than 3,000 decisions, many of which can affect a child's emotions and motivation.[2] Some decisions are large and weigh heavily. For example, the mother of one of Lindsey's students had just died a few days earlier but the girl was back at school. How much should she be encouraged to keep up with the regular pace and how much leeway should she be given to not participate? Decisions like these can be made ahead of time with the counsel of school psychologists and administrators; many more must be made on the fly in the classroom.

Among the most important decisions Lindsey finds herself making repeatedly is whether or not to let a child struggle. For new teachers especially, the urge can be to give too much help, to rush in with the answer or with much of it. A nurturer by nature, Lindsey knows she has to keep this instinct in check and allow students to experience confusion, become more comfortable with it, and learn to problem-solve their way out of it. During the fraction lesson, she reminded her students of the benefits of "Struggle Time," a term she had borrowed from another teacher. The 3rd-graders were required to attempt to solve each problem first on their own, then work collaboratively as a table, sharing strategies, before asking Lindsey for help.

Although she only graduated from her education program a few years ago, the Common Core is so new that Lindsey has had to learn its standards and methods on the job alongside the veteran teachers. She's been pleased with the professional development the school provided to get ready to implement the new standards, which have necessitated some new methods. Her only issue so far has been with the Common Core math: She has found talented students struggling for the first time with the subject, some to a dispiriting extent. One complaint about the Common Core is that it was not phased in, starting in 1st grade and moving up with that class. Instead, students and teachers in every grade through high school were suddenly being held to new standards and expected to learn and teach in new ways that could be antithetical to methods they'd been using for years.[3]

Overall, though, Lindsey seemed optimistic about the changes. She hoped that the new Core-based PARCC (Partnership for Assessment of Readiness for College and Careers) test would better assess than did the existing state test how well students know the material. The PARCC test requires students to write out *how* they solved a math problem and at times requires that they show two different strategies for solving a problem.

This multiple-strategy method, meant to provide conceptual understanding, can be laborious and time-consuming, as we observed during the fractions lesson when Lindsey called different students up to the board to illustrate their various methods of answering the word problem "I have 12 marbles in my collection. I want to give my friend half of them." Lindsey's budding mathematicians are led to understand that there are multiple ways to get to a single answer, and those who need repetition are getting its benefit; on the other hand, it was easy to see how the process could confuse struggling students and bore advanced ones. In fact, Lindsey told us, "Some of the higher students are actually struggling with it more because math was so automatic for them before and now they have to actually take some steps back." These students were asking, "What do you mean I have to tell you why four times five is 20? It is." Some were ready for more challenging material, and now math has suddenly become tedious; they felt they were being asked to do make-work, risking nipping their interest in the subject in the bud. Not all time spent struggling is constructive Struggle Time.

* * *

Since she was 6 years old, Lindsey McClintock has wanted to teach. She spoke to us in glowing terms about the attentive and nurturing teacher she'd had in 1st grade. Inspired by this idol, Lindsey started babysitting at a young age and was volunteering in elementary school classrooms by high school. Long before she had to choose a college, she knew she would major in education. In 2010 she graduated from Arizona State University with several internships and student teaching experiences under her belt and a state teacher's certificate in her pocket.

Graduating into the midst of the Great Recession was a challenge. Teachers were being laid off across the state, and Lindsey and her fellow graduates had to compete for jobs with these newly unemployed veterans. She cast her net wide across Phoenix's sprawl, and though Litchfield Park was 45 minutes from her home on the east side, she took an interview there. Lindsey was delighted by Litchfield Elementary's beautiful campus and welcoming staff, so when the principal called with the job offer, she eagerly accepted, despite a commute that would require setting the alarm for 5:00 a.m.

Her instincts were good. She told us, "Once I started working here, I just fell more in love with it. There is a sense of a community; everybody works together to help each other out. The teams lesson plan together. It's very much a joint effort, and the school's philosophy is that all of the students are our students. That you don't just focus on the 28 in your class." This sense of community extends to the town and the parents, some of whom attended the school as children themselves. Young Lindsey had landed a plum position, a spot in a highly rated school in one of Phoenix's affluent suburbs.

One of the benefits of working in such a district is a high level of parental involvement, shown to have a positive impact on student achievement.[4] Attending parent conferences and checking homework are some of the beneficial kinds of involvement typical of Litchfield Elementary parents. Children from middle- and upper-class households have, among other advantages, a greater likelihood of having a parent at home when they return from school and parents with jobs that allow flexibility to attend school events.

But not every form of involvement by a parent in the school or a child's schooling is helpful. It was a subset of parents in districts like Lindsey's who led to the coinage of the term "helicopter parents." Parents who are overinvolved and "try to advance their children's achievement in a transactional manner" have been shown to reduce children's overall well-being, increase their anxiety, and increase their use of prescription anxiety and pain medication.[5]

While Lindsey sees just a fraction of parents as overinvolved, that small percentage can make big demands, too often with the attitude, she says, that she is a "servant" at their beck and call. Emails at 8:30 p.m. insisting that she call them "right away!" or emails with bulleted lists of requests ("Can you make sure so-and-so turns this in; he has trouble remembering his homework. Can you unpack his bag for him?"), lists that leave Lindsey wishing that parents would remember there are 27 other students in the class.

This imperiousness, Lindsey believes, springs from a poor opinion of the profession and a grave misunderstanding about a teacher's workload. "I think a lot of them do look at me as if I get out at 2:30 and have all the free time in the world and why can't I just sit at home and cater to their requests?" (She felt fortunate she hadn't experienced anything as nasty as had a colleague: When a parent 90 minutes late to get her child after school was asked to try to meet pickup times, the parent blew up. "What the eff do you have to do with your time that's so important that you can't watch my child for an hour?")

Parental involvement may be a double-edged sword, but there are tangible benefits that come from working in a wealthier district. As a result of our nation's inequitable system of funding schools, those in wealthier areas tend to offer higher pay; serve higher-achieving students; have fewer discipline problems; and provide better working conditions for teachers, including smaller class sizes.[6] Arizona's funding formula—how the state distributes funding across districts relative to student poverty—is about average for the nation, earning it a C for this element of funding fairness in a recent report.[7] And so Lindsey's classes are smaller than those of her sister who teaches in a poorer district across Phoenix.

Budget cuts during the recession spared no district, however, including Litchfield Park's. Despite an improving economy, many states have continued providing less funding per student than they had earlier in the 2000s, normalizing emergency levels of spending.[8] Class sizes have consequently grown. While debate continues about the impact of class size on student achievement, few educators would find a 3rd-grade class of 28 optimal. Moreover, the key study to date on class size showed improvement when early grade class sizes were reduced from what its researchers called "regular" class sizes of 22–23.[9]

At the same time, cuts to support staff have added to teachers' nonteaching duties. The crossing guard position at Litchfield Elementary, for example, was eliminated, and now teachers take turns managing traffic to keep kids safe on their way to and from school. (For a bit of perspective, no hospital would replace a parking garage attendant with a rotation of nurses to cut costs.)

When Lindsey got going on the subject of how new work has been loaded on while the hours in a day remain stubbornly at 24, well, she got going. "Every few weeks we have morning duty; we are either on the parking lot or on the playground. Then twice a week we have cafeteria and recess duty. Which gives us, on days that we don't have duty, a 40-minute lunch.

On days that we do, we have 20 minutes. So we're trying to run, go to the bathroom. One time I actually ate a sandwich while using the restroom! There are times when I've had two prep periods a week." The loss of prep time during school hours adds to the hours spent at home planning, grading, and answering emails. Importantly, it reduces Lindsey's ability to collaborate with colleagues, to provide extra help on site, or to teach as effectively in the waning hours of the school day.

It also helps explain why it is so hard to stay healthy. An entire day will go by and she will realize that she hasn't taken a sip from her water bottle. There's no time to feel thirsty.

Not all the recently added work is the result of budget cuts; some is caused by the ever-greater focus on test results. Each week, Lindsey must pull students who have done poorly on benchmark assessments of reading fluency and are deemed at risk of failing the annual standardized tests, and test them to see how many words they can read per minute.

American teachers are being made to work harder—not smarter—than their counterparts in other industrialized nations. They devote 7 hours more a week to their jobs than the average of these countries' teachers.[10] They also devote significantly more hours a week to directly instructing children than do teachers in any other industrialized country—42% more. Lindsey pled on her colleagues' behalf, "I wish policymakers would realize that they are just throwing more and more on us, and because we are people pleasers, because we are passionate about our jobs, we'll just do it. But we're getting burned out. We're getting very burned out. I passed out from exhaustion, dehydration already this year."

Even the most plum job in teaching, one in a district with a relatively healthy tax base, supportive administrators, collaborative colleagues, involved parents, and motivated students, doesn't seem so plum.

* * *

It was one of those days of the 20-minute lunch, after which we joined Lindsey on recess duty. It was a lovely 70-degree Arizona winter's day. The school's outdoor space was generous, with basketball, four square, and tetherball courts and a baseball field and other grassy areas. Children were fanned out all over. It was hard not to anticipate someone falling down, being smacked with a ball, or getting into a tussle or any of the umpteen small calamities that can occur when children play; the teacher's fear, of course, is that something larger will unfold or escalate because of a split second of inattention. This day, though, the drama was comedy rather than tragedy. A panting trio of girls ran up to Lindsey with breaking news: "Miles is chasing people around with a dead caterpillar skin!" We thought our eyes had been everywhere, but only then did they land on Miles, running with his arm outstretched like a cartoon character, wreaking havoc in the outfield. As Lindsey went to put an end to this timeless moment, we were reminded that being a teacher has always been unpredictable and has never been easy.

Nevertheless, the numbers of teachers leaving the profession is high, and the percentage of new teachers leaving is even higher. According to the National Commission on Teaching and America's Future, an estimated one-third of all new teachers leave the profession after 3 years and 46% leave inside of 5. These statistics are alarming. Attrition, which is much higher in teaching than in other fields, is costly.[11] One recent estimate put the direct financial cost to the nation at $2.2 billion.[12]

Each teacher's reasons for quitting can be as complex and layered as were his or her reasons for entering the profession. Nevertheless, setting aside involuntary ones (such as layoffs) and the frequent personal ones (such as the desire to stay home with a baby), the reasons why teachers quit tend to fall into three categories: pay and status, training and development, and working conditions.[13]

Richard Ingersoll, perhaps the nation's foremost researcher on teacher turnover, has cited working conditions as the leading reason why we are losing too many teachers.[14] *Working conditions* is a kitchen sink category, including more than length of the official workday and of the school year. It includes factors that can make it easier or harder for a teacher to teach well, such as how much prep time is provided, how large class sizes are, whether aides are provided, what nonteaching duties are required, how much paperwork is required, what expectations for summer or after-hours work are, and what teaching materials and resources are provided. This last item is also a financial issue; as noted in the Bridgeport case, America's teachers annually spend hundreds of their own dollars for classroom supplies.[15]

Lindsey stated, "I'm almost glad it's not a high-paying job because I wouldn't want people coming to it just for the money, not caring about the kids and just trying to get their paycheck. I do it because I love the kids. Because I love watching them grow. Because I want to be a big part of their lives." She always knew teaching was not a lucrative career—no surprises there. She didn't mind that she'd have to live with roommates for a while.

What she does mind is the financial stress layered on by the merit pay system under which she works. As we saw in the Gilbert case, merit pay plans differ but can produce more anxiety than improvement in teachers. In 2010, Arizona passed legislation requiring that school districts base part of their pay on whether teachers achieve goals that include students' academic growth.[16] In June, Lindsey would receive a lump payment of between $1,500 and $4,000 partly determined by her 3rd-graders' standardized test scores. This end-of-the-year "bonus," she explained, is critical to her livelihood, since she isn't paid over the summer. "This time of year I always get really nervous. I don't want to make it about money because it's not that, but at the same time I do have to still pay rent and make my car payments in June and July. So I try to save a little from each paycheck in preparation in case I don't make it. It is stressful." She understands why this leads some teachers to devote class time to test prep, but "that so goes against what I believe in. They're not here to practice filling in bubbles all day long, that's not what school should be."

Sadly, the teachers, new and veteran, who are prematurely leaving the profession include many who say they love teaching. This is one reason why polls that show relatively high job satisfaction among teachers may be misleading. What they love is their students, their communities, their colleagues, the art and craft of teaching. Dig an inch deeper, though, and teachers' dissatisfactions come to the fore, dissatisfactions that, depending on the school and the teacher, can overwhelm the positive considerations. You can love teaching but not be willing to do a job that makes teaching unlovable or living untenable.

Still, we were surprised when toward the end of our interview Lindsey revealed she was preparing to leave the profession. Although not ready then to declare her exit definitively, she was already enrolled in a graduate school program to become a private counselor, a field where the income is higher, the respect afforded practitioners is greater, and children can be helped to grow in meaningful ways. We probably shouldn't have been too shocked. Asked what she saw as education's purpose, she had replied, "It goes way beyond teaching them how to read or teaching them how to count or add or spell. You want to give them the academic skills to be successful but also social behavior skills to be decent human beings and citizens." Yet her days were filled to the brim with academics. The human part of teaching was smaller than she thought it would be.

* * *

After lunch and recess, it was time for, yes, more math. Lindsey had run out of time before the lunch bell to finish the fraction lesson, so it was time for students to work individually on a worksheet meant to assess their understanding. We were reminded of Ulla Tervo-Desnick's desire to continue teaching 1st grade, where the day could include more than just the tested subjects of reading and math.

We looked up at the agenda Lindsey had written on the board at the beginning of the day. Remaining there was a poetry reading and a social studies lesson. Lindsey had been excited about the social studies lesson she had planned, a lesson introducing the three branches of government that included a quick, fun activity making tri-limbed trees out of aluminum foil. She had described this to us the day before as emblematic of the type of teaching she had looked forward to when she graduated. Understanding that more school time was being devoted to the tested subjects, her education professors had driven home how important it was not to sideline science and social studies. And they had given her a strategy she was excited about:

thematic, hands-on units within which science or social studies content could be covered while the children were practicing math or reading and writing skills.

As the 3rd-graders took their turns at a microphone reading aloud poems they had chosen, it became clear that the reading would continue right up to the moment when Lindsey would have to take her class to a schoolwide assembly that would end the day. The democracy lesson would have to wait. Maybe next week.

*   *   *

Only months after our visit, on the first day of school at Litchfield Elementary, Lindsey posted a Facebook message for her colleagues, wishing them a wonderful new year. Although she promised to visit and bring them their favorite take-out coffee to keep them going, she wouldn't be back.

Questions for Discussion

- How can education schools prepare teachers for the realities of the job, especially when reforms mean these realities are in flux?
- What are teachers learning as they implement the Common Core standards? Is there room for teachers to improve upon them based on experience with various student groups?
- What strategies can teachers use to achieve a healthy work–life balance? What working conditions should they advocate for?
- To increase public awareness of the demands of teaching, can the invisible work teachers do such as planning and grading be made visible?
- What are the most productive types of parental involvement?

Suggestions for Further Reading

Barnes, G., Crowe, E., and Schaefer, B. "The Cost of Teacher Turnover in Five School Districts: A Pilot Study" (National Commission on Teaching and America's Future, 2007).

Hill, N. E., and Tyson, D. F. "Parental Involvement in Middle School: A Meta-analytic Assessment of the Strategies That Promote Achievement." *Developmental Psychology,* 49, no. 3 (2009): 740–763.

Johnson, S. K., Ryser, G. R., and Assouline, S. G. *A Teacher's Guide to Using the Common Core State Standards with Mathematically Gifted and Advanced Learners* (Prufrock, 2013).

Robinson, K., and Harris, A. *The Broken Compass: Parental Involvement with Children's Education* (Harvard University Press, 2013).

TALIS 2013 Results: An International Perspective on Teaching and Learning (OECD, 2014).

Stacey Harrell

chapter 7

Immigration Nation

Teaching the New America in a Charter School

(Lemon Grove, California)

There's more than a little yellow in Lemon Grove, California. At the downtown restaurant where we lunched, yellow flowers topped yellow-oilcloth-covered tables, and a trellis dotted with plastic lemons ran up the wall. Down the street at the main intersection, an enormous lemon sat atop a stone pedestal boasting the town has the "best climate on earth."

Lemon Grove began as an agricultural boomtown, its citrus groves planted mile upon mile at the turn of the 20th century, enabled by a new railroad that moved the area's fruit easily to market. In the early 19th century, before the U.S. Army pushed the border farther south during the Mexican–American War, the area was part of Mexico. World War II and the subsequent Cold War military–industrial boom of San Diego saw the lemon farms plowed under for housing tracts, and now many Lemon Grove residents drive or take the light rail into San Diego, 8 miles west, for work each day.

Perhaps the most significant piece of Lemon Grove history—one with national educational implications—unfolded in 1931. That year, over 20 years before Brown confronted his board of education in Topeka, Mexican families in town fought America's first successful school desegregation battle. The story began at the start of a January school day when Jerome Green, principal of Lemon Grove Elementary, stood in the school's doorway and redirected the 75 Mexican and Mexican American students (of the 169 students enrolled) to a two-room building the school board of trustees had designated for them. Their sudden expulsion came in the context of intensified anti-immigrant and anti-Mexican sentiment as immigration increased through the 1920s and the early days of the Depression.

Lemon Grove's Mexican parents organized themselves and commissioned lawyers to sue the school board, arguing it had "no legal right or power to exclude [the students] from receiving instruction upon an equal basis."[1] Student Roberto Alvarez was designated as the plaintiff. The Superior Court of California ruled in favor of the parents, and their children were soon returned to their regular classrooms.

Educational institutions have long been key settings for debates about equality of opportunity, race, and good citizenship in America. That is partly because schools are the first and sometimes only place where Americans gather in one institution to accomplish something of joint concern. Through schools, public efforts and resources are applied toward human development and opportunity, fueled by the belief that the future can be imagined via a cultivated path that each child should and can take. It is the institution most likely to claim that its purpose is to serve everyone, not just some. Those ideas are both on display and in contention today in charter schools.

Once we'd passed some cacti and slightly peaked palm trees out front and through the wrought-iron security gate of Lemon Grove's Liberty Charter High School ("A Literacy First Charter School"), and once we'd obeyed the bilingual instruction that "visitors must sign in at office (no exceptions, please)," and once we'd entered the school's courtyard, we came upon a teenage oasis. Liberty Charter is a small world that is both like every other American high school—a buzzing hive of adolescents—and different from most any other. Just miles from the border with Mexico, it is a young school on a sunny campus where many students walking between buildings are refugees from global hot spots. But even in its distinctiveness, Liberty Charter tells a story of American education that continues to unfold similarly elsewhere, a story of the struggles to incorporate a remarkably diverse nation.

Dr. Stacey Harrell met us at the main office. Her long, curly brown hair was swept practically to the side and clipped with a barrette, but that barrette sparkled; her black blouse and denim skirt said work, but her dangly orange bracelet and shiny patent leather sandals said play. Outgoing but down-to-earth, she immediately seemed as much Stacey as Dr. Harrell.

Entering teaching 20 years ago, she could not have foreseen the diverse career she's already had. She spent 5 years with 2nd-graders, then a few years teaching math and art in middle and high school, and 6 years at a private Christian academy. While she's also been an administrator, "there was too much paperwork and too little relating to students, too much policing and not enough supporting and encouraging." Each of these experiences has fed into how she teaches today, with her time as an elementary school teacher helping her, for example, to teach the whole child, to "home in on all of your kids' aspects."

Although she started on the usual route into education, getting her BA and teaching credentials at a local college, she did so as a first-generation college student for whom such a future was no foregone conclusion. Stacey sees her personal history as demonstrating the promise of education as uplift. "I grew up in a poor, single-mom family, and I see what education has done for me. It is very powerful, and it can change your life." While working and raising a son on her own, she went on further, obtaining her PhD in education. She now changes the lives of the life-changers, instructing teachers-in-training at the local community college at night after a full day at Liberty. She does this to pay off loans from that advanced-degree work, and because the long hours, she claimed, help her "sleep well."

It wasn't long into her teaching career that Stacey developed grander ambitions: She wanted to create her own school. With a group of colleagues from the private school where she worked, she left to establish a place where, she said emphatically, "*all* kids will be helped to be successful, not just some." One source of this passion was her own dyslexia, which led her "to identify with the kids who struggled" to learn. She wanted to teach in a school that focused, as Liberty's mission statement claims, on cultural literacy, parent involvement (a striking 40 hours of volunteer time a year are requested), "passionate" and individual child-centered teaching, and the use of advanced technology. She and her fellow founders also wanted to instill notions of good character and encourage community service. Finally, they wanted to use the latest educational research to design their practices, rather than be forced to rely on methods that "a textbook company" had determined were best.

Liberty Charter opened with 100 students and five teachers in a rented building in nearby El Cajon. Some of the first students came from the local Chaldean Catholic community, a religious refugee group that had first come to Southern California from Iraq in the 1990s, then in larger waves after the U.S. invasion and after immigration restrictions were loosened in 2007. The school opened, unfortunately, in 2001. In the climate of fear and recrimination following the 9/11 attacks that put Arab-speaking, Middle Eastern–looking Americans at risk, some students traveled to school with police patrols. The silver lining: "We got a lot of bonding at that moment."

Other students were the children of home schooling parents attracted to the school's mission statement, including some who had exited traditional public schools, feeling their children needed more attention than they were getting. The school kept growing; when we visited, 400 students were enrolled in four grades. Five hundred more sat on their waiting list.

When Stacey and her colleagues applied for charter school status and funding, California was, she said, "not charter friendly." With a wave of advocacy, the tide has turned. While Liberty was the first charter school in San Diego County when it was incorporated in 2008, the county now lists 121. Nationally, roughly 6,000 charter schools are estimated to be in operation, a still relatively small fraction (6%) of all public schools but a growing one, particularly in cities.[2] While charter schools are public schools insofar as they receive public funding and are free to students, freedom from the constraints they see imposed in existing public schools–and seen most starkly in the Litchfield Park case–is something their advocates celebrate. For charter schools that are not unionized (only 12% are, though the figure is growing), the length of the school day and school year, for example, are not subject to contract negotiations.[3] Liberty Charter's day runs an extra hour; its 8:15 to 3:30 school day provides time for the basics as well as for music and gardening. Liberty is unusual in this; while the extension of teaching time has been a central goal of school reform movements, just 10% of charter schools had extended time in 2009–2010.[4] Charters can also pay teachers less, allowing for cost savings that can reduce class sizes (Liberty Charter's classes are sized well below the state average), provide funding for technology, or simply operate within tight budgets. Charter schoolteachers earn $9,100 less on average than their counterparts in traditional public schools, who, as discussed in the Gilbert and Litchfield Park cases, themselves can struggle to make ends meet.[5]

Stacey acknowledged that she is paid less than other public school teachers in the area, but she finds balancing considerations. She feels she has greater opportunities for collaboration and collegiality than she would otherwise. She also enjoys what she considers high levels of trust in her judgment about how to teach, rather than "being told to be on this page [of the textbook] on this day." Some teachers in charter schools feel they have a greater ability to develop curriculum and use new methods than do teachers in some traditional public schools, although the difference between their feelings and their curricula and those of public school teachers may not be great.[6]

Like many charter school teachers and administrators, Stacey and her colleagues are master multitaskers. As both a cost-saving matter and an identity matter, teachers in charters often wear multiple hats: teachers, advisors, and administrators. Stacey uses her background in educational psychology to work as a counselor some days after school.

Despite the rigor and fullness of her day, Stacey shares the view of many teachers that the public "thinks we don't work very hard." Asked whether she believes she receives more or less respect than her peers in traditional public schools, she thought not. Like them, she grates when tossed the rhetorical question "Wouldn't it be nice to have the summer off?" or the rhetorical challenge "I am paying your salary."

* * *

Stacey teaches math at Liberty. The attitude she cultivates chirps in bright-blue lettering across one of her bulletin boards: "Mathiness is happiness." She's stapled other signs there that serve as both math *and* life lessons: "Make sense of problems and persevere in solving them"; "Attend to precision"; "Look for and make use of structure." Explicit character and behavior admonitions hang from the ceiling on cardboard disks: "Show self-discipline and keep your emotions, words, and actions under control!" "Be caring and think about the needs of others!" "Be a good citizen at home, at school, and in your community!"

The room broadcasts that this is a particularly *American* classroom, with community values in careful balance with individualism. Collage self-portraits of students adorn the walls, advertising their unique identities. Then there is the deck of cards on Stacey's desk, cards printed with messages such as "Please don't bug me, I'm having a bad day" that students can use on occasion to cut themselves off from the pack. Students' sense of being "loved and known" as individuals in the classroom is a characteristic of the school that Stacey thinks students and their parents appreciate.

Stacey teaches students from the remedial to the advanced and from freshmen to seniors. She teaches descendants of families that have lived in California since the 19th century and students born in Iraq and Myanmar, some of whom struggle to translate from their first languages to the English of their instruction. In just one class, she may have students whose first languages are Tagalog, Arabic, Karen, Thai, or Spanish. These are often students who have been through the trauma of war.

The day is a rigorous 7-plus hours, with just 5 minutes to pass between periods, and a quick 25 minutes for lunch in the courtyard under big umbrellas at aquamarine picnic tables. Students come from a large catchment area, some from as far as 20 miles away. They get to school by carpool, trolley, and public bus, some traveling as much as 2 hours each way.

Eighteen students, uniformed and backpacked, filed into Stacey's first class, prealgebra. Mateo, Charlotte, Jasmine, Brent, and the others took their places at six separate tables. Stacey started with a practical mini-lesson in buying fast food, opening with a clip from *The Pink Panther* in which Steve Martin expresses his flamboyantly French-accented desire to "buy a haamburrrger." She handed out worksheets of "Menu Math," in which an h symbolized a hamburger and an s a soda, and encouraged them to work out the prices of each item if $2h + 3s = \$5.15$. She reminded them to "be precise, especially with money, because you can lose money." In the wake of the school reforms—initially conservative but now more neoliberal—launched across the country in the 1980s, she and many other teachers see their job as one in which they must give students knowledge that will shape, not just mind or character, but also their "economic competitiveness in a changing marketplace."[7]

After they'd worked on the problem on their own, she asked them to work with the others at their table. The emphasis on teamwork continued in the next section of prealgebra, where the children were instructed not to proceed to the worksheet's second page until their entire table was ready to move on: "We can't leave a teammate behind." At that prompt, Jasmine turned to Gabriel, still working on page 1, and asked if he'd like some help. After a second's hesitation, he asked Jasmine a specific question about the process of solving the equation.

Emotional support and mutual aid were central features of Stacey's classroom climate. In one class, Shawna, a girl with dangling earrings and khakis tucked into boots, was struggling as the others finished, but Stacey asked her to remember what they had done the other day. After a few queries from Stacey, Shawna had figured it out and checked her work. To reinforce the lesson for everyone, Stacey announced, "I like that you double-checked your work before you continued." She soon told Joseph, also for all to hear, "That's a great strategy, putting circles and boxes around the things you are focused on. I use that strategy all the time."

By the end of each class, she had called on almost everyone for ideas on how to solve the day's problem. And Shawna, her earrings flashing, turned to her friend in the next seat and exclaimed, "I'm so smart today!" To drive home the expansive point, smiling wide, she drew two big jazz hand circles in midair.

In a section of upperclassmen later that day, mutual support and assistance was also on display. Alexa was frustrated by not being able to get her addition correct for one problem. She laid her head sideways on the desk and kept it there until Stacey came by to prompt her through the sticky problem. Another girl at the table, a beauty sporting a big purple hair bow, reassured her, "You're doing good, Alexa. You're doing good."

Setting an easy atmosphere for the not-so-easy work, Stacey plugged in a cinnamon-scented air freshener and put on soft baroque background music as the students toiled over their four pages of practice. A key goal was to muffle the distractions of conversations at other tables and create an optimal learning environment.

A focus of urban charter schools has been reducing distractions through discipline ranging from the mild to the controversially strict.[8] When they finished their sheets, the prealgebra students waited patiently and quietly for everyone to be done, just one example of evidence of expectations for behavior at Liberty. Infractions of standards occur, of course, but are handled swiftly and consistently. When a boy walked into one class tossing out a swearword, Stacey informed him quietly, "You'll be cleaning for me today." At the end of class, though he tried to slip outside, Stacey put him to work washing down each of the room's six tables, which he did with surprising cheerfulness.

As a cofounder, Stacey was involved in key decisions about discipline at the school's founding, including requiring uniforms. Liberty students must wear khaki, black, or navy-blue pants or plaid skirts and two- or three-button polo shirts in one of nine colors; they are prohibited from wearing hats, clothing with labels or logos other than the school logo, or sagging pants or leggings. These sartorial limits, she said, help the school "keep the main thing the main thing." Limits are pushed nonetheless: Victor came into class clutching his backpack awkwardly to his chest, a tip-off that his sweatshirt might have featured illicit text. At Stacey's request, he was soon wearing it inside out.

When a student in a remedial class was caught riling up his table, she took him outside to talk rather than shame him in front of peers. Some students misbehave as a kind of escape when the work of the moment becomes too difficult, and this seemed a likely cause here. In this class, Stacey had to be even more diligent about getting to each table, prodding and helping. She also made clear, though, that any unfinished classwork would become homework that night. These firm but humane disciplinary actions provided a contrast to some of the more controversial, even severe, discipline reported at certain charters that has led policy researchers to look critically at the way they affect school culture and student achievement.[9]

Stacey instructed all students to take out planners and write down their homework, but in this class she required them to show her the completed item in their planner before they could be dismissed. This attention to assignment bookkeeping is but one example of how much teaching time now goes into scaffolding study skills, something less in evidence in classrooms of the 1950s or 1960s. In the past, by high school, the teacher taught content and the student was responsible for learning it; failure was attributed to lack of student motivation.[10] Rising inequality, geographic mobility, and diversity meant that American teachers could no longer assume that all students possessed the same basic study skills. With the 1975 passage of the precursor law to the Individuals with Disabilities Education Act (IDEA), teachers and schools were also expected to do more to help all students succeed; IDEA ushered in an era in which differentiating for individual learning styles and abilities became the expectation for schools, not the exception. Less parental time for children's homework supervision in a context of longer workweeks for both parents has also transformed what were once considered parent responsibilities into teacher duties. Layered on this is the rise of a testing system in which schools and teachers, not students and parents, are held accountable when yearly standards aren't met or exceeded.

Stacey's biggest frustration as a teacher is not the helicopter parents who plague some other teachers but "parents not doing their jobs," a failure that has ramifications every day for her success in doing her job. While their great asset at Liberty Charter, she believes, is that parents and students "have chosen our school," there is a small percentage of parents—5%, she guesses—who are neglectful or "borderline abusive," telling their children that they are "stupid" or not providing them with enough food. The school then becomes, she says, the one place these young people find safety and support.

Although she did not put it exactly this way, Stacey's unhappiness stems from the larger social order not doing its job, either—half of Liberty Charter students are on free and reduced-price lunch. Many need vouchers to help them buy their uniforms. A broader social push to alleviate poverty would certainly help Stacey achieve her main goal of creating "value-conscious thinkers" who are "literate citizens" of that society.

Charter schools skew more urban than other public schools to a strong degree.[11] They emerged there in a context of great inequality of educational outcomes between rich and poor, White and non-White. The early school choice movement was motivated in part by a desire to circumvent court-ordered desegregation and underpinned by a conservative cultural logic that called for privatizing public schools in the interest of allowing market forces to close bad schools and improve quality in others.[12] At this point, charter school teachers are much more likely than those in public schools to have non-Whites in their classrooms; Black and Hispanic students make up 57% of the population in charter schools versus 38% of the student population in noncharter public schools.[13] The quality or outcomes debate aside, critics have noted that the racial segregation of charter schools has increased even more sharply than that of public schools more generally.[14]

However, over time, the movement has attracted more participants with aspirations for greater racial equality in educational outcomes. Some charter school advocates see it as "America's new civil rights movement."[15] Just as Stacey expressed her hopes that Liberty Charter would provide opportunity for all, many teachers choose to work in charter schools because they value the chance to advantage the disadvantaged as "part of a larger movement."[16] At the same time, critics point to research showing outcomes in charters overall are often no better, and sometimes worse, than in traditional public schools. They also highlight cases in which for-profit charter schools have paid their owners too handsomely with public monies and in which even not-for-profit charters have allowed abuse of public funds or outright fraud.[17] In addition, a coalition of civil rights groups, including the NAACP and the National Urban League, has sharply criticized the Race to the Top initiative. They claim the program, which incentivizes states to expand charter schools, close neighborhood schools, and use a competitive funding formula, disadvantages low-income and minority students.[18]

*   *   *

At the closing bell, this debate felt distant as the school's United Nations of students joyfully flowed off the school grounds. While minorities would form the majority of America's public schoolchildren by the 2014–2015 school year, the only students who appeared underrepresented at Liberty Charter were White ones.[19] Other high schools in the district have a different racial makeup: Three-quarters of Santana High School's students are non-Hispanic Whites, but only 16% of Mount Miguel High's students are. American classrooms across the nation remain almost as segregated today as they were before the civil rights movements of the 1950s and 1960s.[20]

The challenge of race in American education was well in evidence during 1931's "Lemon Grove incident." Declaring the segregation of Mexican American students illegal, the presiding judge ruled that the school "immediately admit and receive the petitioner, Roberto Alvarez, and all other pupils of Mexican parentage . . . that they be admitted to said school on a basis of equality . . . without separation or segregation."[21]

In the judge's rationale, however, is a taste of the ironies and contradictions that have characterized the American search for educational equity. His decision rested on a technicality: that the 1848 Treaty of Guadalupe Hidalgo had classified Mexicans as Caucasian. It was that precedent, not the ideal of a classroom that welcomed everyone, that prevented Lemon Grove's school district from discriminating as it had been.[22]

Questions for Discussion

- How is the experience of teachers in charter schools distinct from that of teachers in other public schools?
- Are some schools, such as charter or magnet, Catholic or other private schools, able to do a better job of keeping art and music teaching in school?
- What responsibilities for children's learning once left to parents should teachers fill?
- When is classroom discipline too strict, and when is it not strict enough?
- What is the role of schools in providing immigrant students with a sense of belonging?

Suggestions for Further Reading

"Discipline Data: Charters vs. Noncharters." *Education Week*, 32, no. 21. Updated May 16, 2013. http://www.edweek.org/ew/section/infographics/charter-discipline-infographic.html

Ravitch, D. *Reign of Error: The Hoax of the Privatization Movement and the Danger to America's Public Schools* (Random House, 2013).

Rothstein, J. M. "Good Principals or Good Peers? Parental Valuation of School Characteristics, Tiebout Equilibrium, and the Incentive Effects of Competition Among Jurisdictions." *American Economic Review*, 96, no. 4 (2006): 1333–1350.

Wie, J., Patel, D., and Young, V. M. "Organizational Differences Between Charter Schools and Traditional Public Schools." *Education Policy Analysis Archives*, 22 (January 2014). http://files.eric.ed.gov/fulltext/EJ1018832.pdf

Wohlstetter, P., Smith, J., and Farrell, C. C. *Choices and Challenges: Charter School Performance in Perspective* (Harvard Education Press, 2013).

Glorianna Under Baggage

chapter 8

Before They Drop
Pointing the Poorest Students Toward Hope

(Kyle, South Dakota)

We flew into Rapid City's trim, newly renovated airport en route to meet Glorianna Under Baggage, a teacher on the Pine Ridge Reservation. Because we blended in with the summer vacationers, the young blond clerk at the car rental counter was primed to recommend sites to us. With the brio of a seasoned tour guide, he directed us first to Mount Rushmore's granite presidential heads. Then, he insisted, we had to check out the 160-mile-deep Jewel Cave, Badlands National Monument, Big Thunder Gold Mine, and the Flintstones Bedrock City Theme Park. Finally, he recommended a scenic drive through the Black Hills.

Carrying this advice and a Convention and Visitors Bureau guide, we headed out into South Dakota. Nowhere in the thick, glossy guide, though, could we find directions to the Pine Ridge Reservation. Nor was there any mention of a monument to the massacre at Wounded Knee, located on the reservation. Textbooks identify the massacre—whose horrors took place on a bitterly cold December 29, 1890—as a key event in U.S. history. It has come to symbolize the end of the bloodletting that facilitated centuries of "Indian removals" and land confiscations; it coincided with Congress's declaration that the frontier's edge had been reached and a chapter of American history closed.[1] We would have to buy a gas station map to get us where we were going.

Although Glorianna is not the only teacher in America whose community has a rich or tragic history, her students live further off the map of national visibility and deeper in the shadow of history than most teens: They are Oglala Lakota (Sioux). The living legacy of history's dispossessions is reflected in the community's poverty, ill health, and mass unemployment, which are more extreme than those of any other community across the continent. More than half of the reservation's population lives below the pitifully low level that the U.S. government calls "poor," and 8 out of 10 of its adults are unemployed.[2] Alcohol and drug addiction are rampant responses to and aggravators of these conditions.

None of these sorrowful facts were visible, though, as we drove onto the reservation. Nothing but mile after mile of softly rolling fields came into

view, their golden yellows and greens so vivid they seemed digitally en-
hanced. Some were dotted with horses or cattle, tail-switching in summer's
heat, and many were punctuated with neat, modest ranch homes set back
from the road with bicycles, trampolines, and grills out front. Only the lone
retail establishment along our route, a gas station convenience store stocked
with Combos, Little Debbies, and Pepsis but little fresh food hinted at the
scant local economy.

There are only a handful of places to eat and sleep if you are visiting
Pine Ridge Reservation and you aren't kin. We did both at the Lakota
Prairie Ranch, where we met Glorianna for an all-American diner lunch
of hamburgers, French fries, and fried dill pickles. Her gray hair, captured
loosely in a long ponytail, framed a face full of the optimism associated
with youth. We were especially grateful that Glorianna met with us that
day, given the fullness of her days and our painful awareness of the old
saying that every Indian family includes parents, grandparents, children,
and an anthropologist.

Before we buckled down to the business of talking about teaching, the
menu's senior citizen discounts got us onto the topic of aging. Our kvetching
about the indignities that accompany such perks led Glorianna to slip into
her teacher voice to set us straight. To be an elder, she gently lectured, is to
enter a stage of great opportunity—an opportunity to teach those who have
come after us and to model the community service we'd like them to pay
forward. There are, she said, distinctive attitudes and responsibilities that
should come with chronological maturity. And they don't include self-pity
or regret. At the cusp of 70, she sees herself as a woman meant to put away
self-centered vanities and pass on her accumulated understanding.

Our lesson continued at the small historical museum housed at Oglala
Lakota College. Glorianna escorted us through the exhibit there before taking us outside for more conversation on the college's powwow grounds,
where just a month earlier the 40th annual OLC graduation ceremony and
powwow had feted 129 graduates.[3] It may be the single most hopeful spot
on the reservation.

* * *

Her marriage to a Lakota brought Glorianna to the Great Plains, but she
was born in San Francisco and reared in the Southwest, an Apache by birth
and upbringing. Her parents taught her to value schooling, and she would
eventually go on to study law and education; however, she was made to
understand she would be "well educated before the first day in school." Before kindergarten, she learned the core values her parents and grandparents
thought essential in a good adult, among them deference to elders, cour-
tesy and respect, and community service. In the classroom, she could expect
to gain knowledge about subjects like math and reading and social studies.

Education, though, was bigger than the sum of these. It was about character, and character was learned in the Indian home. Schooling was about skill building, and in both senses, it came second.

Glorianna worries that some Native students arrive in high school now lacking pieces of this fundamental family education. It is her hope and faith that as a teacher, she can help put those pieces in place by the time they graduate. "I wanted to capture some time with them before they went into adulthood," she said. "So if there were messages that they had not received, instruction that they had not gotten, understandings that they didn't have, maybe I would be able to catch that moment and give them that."

Little Wound High School, in an impressive red-tiled building constructed in the shape of a buffalo's head, sits on Main Street in Kyle, one of a handful of small towns on the reservation. Glorianna arrived there after winding a decades-long path through a seemingly diverse set of jobs. She didn't always understand these as teaching jobs, though now she realizes they all had, at their core, reaching the young. They also all involved the work of cultural repair and the mission of inspiration.

Losing her first child at 20 may have been the dark impetus that set Glorianna on her journey. Unable to bring another pregnancy to term, she struggled to recover from the terrible loss she felt in not having the chance to become someone's "first teacher." Eventually, she came to see that an equally valuable position could be hers as an "auntie" or "grandmother," which "in the Indian way" a woman can become even if she hasn't borne children.

An early job providing this role was as leader of Victim-Offender Reconciliation, a nonprofit she founded to serve people broken by crime. Applying her legal and mediation skills to achieve what is called restorative justice, she brought people who had been convicted of harming others together with their victims. The goal was to help heal victims, but also to teach perpetrators, often quite young, how to rethink their behavior and try to repair the damage they had done.

She first worked with Indian youth on California's central coast. Especially moving was the plight of one young man who had suffered permanent brain damage from alcohol poisoning; he wistfully remembered that he was once bright. Another boy, who had started smoking pot at age 5, was still unable, as an 8-year-old, to read or concentrate. Glorianna prodded him to start running; slowly clearing his lungs and mind, he went on to win a long-distance race, an achievement that crystallized his break from drugs.

Her next jobs involved alcohol and drug counseling with Indian youth, family violence prevention, and parent education, where she helped young adults enact the positive values they had been raised with but had abandoned. After these years of nontraditional teaching, she finally made her way into a classroom, working with a local college's service-learning program. Here, she said, "I learned how much young people don't realize the importance of their involvement in a community—because young people aren't valued in that way. And that's our error as adults: not showing them their importance as contributing members of our society." She came to see teaching as an "honor" and see herself as especially suited to it "later in life," when she "had something of value maybe to offer."

She moved to Pine Ridge and, in 2011, came to work at Little Wound High School (in the Lakota language, Taopi Cikala Owayawa). The school's mission statement is to "provide a sacred environment for students to achieve academic and Lakota language and cultural excellence." Although good teacher–student ratios do not always translate to good outcomes, this school has the advantage of 35 staff, including 24 teachers, for 275 students.[4] As elsewhere in rural America but especially in Indian country, the students don't experience a sharp separation between home and school; they likely have relatives among the students and the staff. A teacher could be a grandmother or a custodian an uncle. So it is that Glorianna relates to her students as both teacher and kin to the latest generations of her husband's extended family.

A central focus of the school, its website notes, is "to provide a learning opportunity reflective of the four major Lakota values of wisdom, generosity, respect, and courage." Although she works in a public school, instilling values is a goal Glorianna shares with Catholic teacher Ann Marie and home schooling parent Heather. She tries to keep her students "mindful that they are Lakota. If they make a comment that is not Lakota in feeling, I will ask them what Lakota values they are instantiating." When we asked how important it was for teachers at her school to be Native, she responded, "If a teacher conducts themselves in a good manner, does what they preach, that is the teacher who will be valued." Identity is important but character trumps it, particularly when, in an intimate rural setting, news of bad behavior spreads fast.

As at many rural schools, students can travel from as far as 50 miles away each day. That challenge aside, a small pond provides better opportunity to be a big fish; 10% of a recent graduating class received the classic high school distinctions: Cree Dawn Iron Cloud was valedictorian, Alyssa Whirlwind Horse was salutatorian, and Jacey Mesteth and Tangerine LeBeau were homecoming king and queen. Dozens more stood out as basketball stars and art award winners.[5]

For all this tradition, Little Wound's virtual classroom, which Glorianna runs, is at the leading edge of education in the 2010s. K–12 virtual education can range from a single computer-based class or lab in an otherwise traditional teaching environment to online programs offering all the credits a student needs to get a high school diploma. In its various forms, virtual education is growing rapidly despite some controversy and limited research into its effectiveness. In some states and districts, virtual classes are popping up in response to squeezed budgets; in others, online education is seen as a way to expand learning by providing students with additional college level course offerings and as a way to especially serve students in rural settings.[6]

Throughout the school day, over the course of seven periods, 20 or so students cycle through Glorianna's room. In a school in which only every other student will graduate, these are the ones especially at risk of dropping out, whether because of pregnancy and early parenthood, failed coursework, illness or injury, or absenteeism. Although students who are sick can work from home if they have a computer, most of her students come into the classroom to work on an online curriculum, completing required courses. A child who has failed algebra, for example, rather than having to sit embarrassedly in that same class again, may be working to solve problems online, with Glorianna there to poke, prod, teach, and reteach. So-called blended learning environments like this have proved effective with academic credit recovery classes.[7] There are also students who take online courses to graduate early. (Glorianna also teaches Publications, which produces the yearbook, and was recently named to head the gifted and talented education program.)

We were somewhat surprised to learn that the Little Wound High School curriculum for academic classes, online and off, must and does conform to both Common Core standards and South Dakota state standards. Despite their nation's sovereign status, South Dakota tribal reservation schools are subject to the same expectations for learning and standardized testing requirements as are the state's public schools—if they want funding, that is. That functional lack of sovereignty and a thin economic base meant reservation schools were disproportionately affected by the 2013 government sequester. While most districts across America get only a sliver of their funding from the federal government, 60% of Pine Ridge's comes from federal sources. Cuts to staff had immediate impact.[8]

Federal involvement in Indian education has had a problematic history. The past includes notorious boarding schools run by the federal government and Christian missionaries in the 19th and 20th centuries. Thousands of Native American children were taken from their families, made to adopt Euro-American hair and clothing styles and other cultural norms, and forbidden to speak their own languages or practice their own religions, all in a purported attempt to civilize them. Some were subject to abuse, both physical and sexual, and to unhealthy, even deadly living conditions. As late as 1973, an estimated 60,000 Native students still attended such schools.[9] Out of this dark history has come a deep commitment to developing a robust on-reservation educational system that incorporates both formal schooling and indigenous cultural revival.

This is a daunting goal. The challenges for reservation schools, including poverty and racism, have translated to educational statistics more dire than those of nearly any other district in the country. High school graduation rates nationally for Native youth, at 68%, are far below the average for all students.[10] The numbers for South Dakota are even worse, with just 42% of all Native American students in the class of 2012 donning a cap and gown—roughly half the state average. Glorianna works with students who are most at risk of becoming a drop-out statistic.

When one of them joined Glorianna's virtual program from another school, she had one infant; when she graduated, a feat that required a lot of school staff support, she had three. Even Glorianna is surprised by how important it has turned out to be to "encourage, encourage, encourage." Research bears out the critical role of positive reinforcement in countering the confluence of such things as personal trauma, poverty, substance abuse, lack of family support, family dysfunction, and peer pressure or alienation that may feed into a student's decision to drop out.[11] We can't give up on the children, Glorianna argued, who "make a left turn when it should have been a right." After all, she believes, they are struggling because of what "we as adults in this world have done." They are suffering as a result of "our failures, our omissions."

Few of her students don't complete the classes they start. But Glorianna does not foster this success by being unrelenting. Her goal of producing "contemplative, thinking young people" who serve their community requires, in her view, rigor but not rigidity. She can't forget the harsh single-mindedness with which her own Catholic schoolteachers pursued the goal of teaching her English-language skills. Glorianna was not permitted to speak her own language in school (quite ironically, as it turns out, since these standard-bearers were European nuns who had never given up their own native French).

Firmness balanced with flexibility became Glorianna's way. This means recognizing that on any given day one or more students may be unable to perform to the standard she seeks. It means leaving emotional space to deal with what is going on in the community. With higher rates of car crashes, suicides, and life-shortening diseases on the reservation than off, it's likely that some number of her students will be rocked by the untimely death of a loved one or a neighbor.[12] More joyfully, flexibility means momentarily easing up on work when students are readying for a Lakota language competition or a basketball tournament and Glorianna sees that "there is nothing more important to them than basketball and we need to acknowledge it."

Flexibility means keeping a stock of healthy foods in her classroom and giving a child who may not have had breakfast a handful of cranberries or a Sweet and Salty bar before launching into science or writing lessons. It means having this typical conversation with a groggy student:

"You look a little tired this morning, did you get enough rest?"

"No."

"How come?"

"I had to watch my younger brothers because my mom and dad weren't there. They had to go and take care of some things."

"Oh, okay. You need some rest, huh? You want some water?"

At this point, she'll hand over the wood-carved eagle feather that constitutes a hall pass.

"Maybe you should get some water, but I'd like you to take the loooong route to the water; don't take the shortcut. Take the long route by the counselor and say hello to him for me."

Glorianna's title at Little Wound when we met her was not classroom teacher but "Odyssey Director," an apt title for a woman who understands that life's journey is rarely a straight line (she is now "EDgenuity Instructor"). The small kindnesses she offers students along their winding ways make up a practical magic. Knowing when to push and when not to push pays off: "If I give them that, in turn they will give me all that they can," she says.

There's no small contrast between this nurturing push-and-pull and the recent insistence of some education reform advocates that children must develop "grit" or the "perseverance to accomplish long-term or higher-order goals in the face of challenges and setbacks, engaging the student's psychological resources, such as their academic mindsets, effortful control, and strategies and tactics."[13] When the "challenges and setbacks" are so profound, demanding "grit" is akin to asking young people who are already white-knuckling life to just buck up. Instead, Glorianna fosters resilience by seeking to instill the Lakota value of courage, an approach that seems not just softer but also more nuanced and likely to be effective; the "noncognitive factors" that can improve student performance are numerous and require, among other things, a feeling of self-worth and strong relationships with adults that foster a sense of belonging.[14]

As the three of us spoke, the sky grayed and for a while a slight, solemn rain fell on the roof sheltering the powwow ground stands. But Glorianna darkened only once—when we asked for her opinion of current school reforms. Sharpening, she questioned whether reform leaders had classroom experience or knowledge of children, and questioned a movement in which testing overtook learning. Truly, she answered herself, this is not the needed type of reform.

"*This* is what we need," she asserted. "Adequate and sufficient amounts of healthy food for all children for breakfast, lunch, and supper. Adequate living accommodations for all children; no longer having to sleep in overcrowded conditions in homes that should be condemned. And that's in the reservation or it's in the inner cities that I'm talking about," she emphasized, speaking on behalf of students in places like Lemon Grove and Bridgeport as well as those in Pine Ridge.

She continued, "Adequate preventative health. Adequate physical education. Kids need this. This is just fundamental stuff. And art and music."

Glorianna's frustration stems from her firsthand knowledge that student achievement, something over which schools have meaningful but limited influence, is profoundly affected by socioeconomic status. A deep body of research has consistently shown that poverty, especially extreme and persistent poverty, has a tremendous and complex impact on children's physical, social, and emotional health; cognitive ability; and resulting academic achievement.[15]

A recurring image came to Glorianna as we spoke, and something seemed to collapse inside, cracking her voice with grief. "Because kids come to school and they put their heads on the table and they are so tired and they are so hungry. How can we have them learn, when we can't even provide them . . ." She paused, and then another image rose up to her, of a teacher or reformer who looks at the child with his head on the desk or his homework undone and *doesn't* see, who says, "Oh, they're being lazy." And then with more fire she launched another volley of questions: "Who are you to judge those children that are suffering? Who are you to judge them when they don't even have a bed in their home? That's what they [the reformers] need to take care of."

She stopped. "I think I said it all."

We turned off the recorder, gathered our things, and walked together back across the campus. The sky was once again a deep Dakota blue.

*   *   *

Earlier that morning, we had driven to Wounded Knee. At roughly the intersection of BIA (Bureau of Indian Affairs) Highway 28 and Bigfoot Trail, we found the memorial to the massacre. A single bright-red sign's hand-painted letters recounted in detail the U.S. Army's forced march of Lakota Sioux men, women, and children to this creek valley and their slaughter of all but one of the 126 of them.

We pulled over into one of the six marked parking spots by the sign and walked down the grassy slope beyond to a collection of wooden arbors overlooking the massacre site. Silence. The assemblage looked both abandoned by the world at large and on profound watch and witness. Back across the highway sat a small family-run museum, the Holocaust Museum at Wounded Knee, where a middle-aged son of the family introduced us to its collection of historic artifacts and photographs, some streaked with water stains from a leaky roof. Leaving the museum, we walked up the hill to the cemetery joined by someone's yellow dog, our every step scattering a spray of grasshoppers across the dusty brush.

There we found a collection of grave markers older and newer, many commemorating lives cut shockingly short. And we met a man in his late 20s, sitting on the stone gate marking the entrance to the cemetery. He laid out a small inventory of tourist goods–a few bead necklaces and a simple suede pouch his grandmother had sewn. He had graduated from high school, we learned, and with the help of Pell grants had taken some classes at the local college. He had been unable to continue school, however, or to find work on the reservation. Although he had been to the local army recruiting office a number of times, he'd had no offer to join up. Still holding out hope, he planned to return to the recruiter.

Pine Ridge's unemployment rate is estimated at 80–90%.[16] Most jobs that do exist are in the schools, tribal government, and hospitals, and almost all require a college degree. The local college system has made some strides. An average of 1,500 to 1,800 students are registered each semester across a decentralized set of nine centers, with many more people taking Lakota language classes.[17] The colleges have gradually increased the number of Lakota with a bachelor's degree; they've prepared most of the teachers and nurses now working at Pine Ridge. But without a tax base and with the failure to refund the 1978 Education Amendments Act, which gave funding and local hiring authority directly to tribal schools, the challenges of educating and graduating Native American are more formidable than ever. The reservation just opened its first local bank, however, and there is hope that this will enable entrepreneurs to create more jobs.

* * *

In light of such a past and such a possible future, it is reasonable to wonder how a Lakota teen can see the value of working hard in the present—and it is reasonable to ask how a teacher who knows the odds can stay motivated.

Glorianna shares reading content and math skills with her students. But the main thing she shares is hope. She came to understand that what her Indian learners need most is "to be continually encouraged and told how hopeful things can be. That message of enthusiasm for life, of hopefulness, and of encouragement is, to me, what is really important."

No other teacher we met better schooled us on that score.

Questions for Discussion

- How does federal and state control of standards affect teachers' ability to teach to community values?
- What responsibility do teachers have to instill hope in their students? Are encouragement and rigor incompatible?
- Dropout prevention is one of the few areas of education upon which there is broad consensus and a willingness to devote resources. Why is this so?
- How can teachers working in districts with profound poverty avoid becoming discouraged? What kind of extra support can these teachers give their students?

Suggestions for Further Reading

Jensen, E. *Teaching with Poverty in Mind: What Being Poor Does to Kids' Brains and What Schools Can Do About It* (Association for Supervision & Curriculum Development, 2009).

Reyhner, J., and Eder, J. *American Indian Education* (University of Oklahoma Press, 2006).

Schargel, F., and Smink, J. *Helping Students Graduate: A Strategic Approach to Dropout Prevention* (Routledge, 2004).

Tough, P. *How Children Succeed: Grit, Curiosity, and the Hidden Power of Character* (Mariner, 2013).

Gary Anderson

chapter 9

From the Page to the Screen

Social Media and High School English

(Palatine, Illinois)

Boone, Iowa, in 1974 was a small town that didn't think it was a small town because it was the county seat and more people lived there than anyplace nearby. Smack in the middle of the state and 20 miles from the interstate, it was small enough to invite a boy with big ideas to get into trouble and not big enough for that trouble to overtake him. That being said, it's unlikely his Boone High teachers expected Gary Anderson, no model student, to follow in their footsteps.

When asked to identify the inspiration for their career choice, teachers tend to reminisce about idols who sparked their passion for a subject or who showed by example that teaching made for a worthwhile life. But it wasn't the stars who prompted young Gary to consider teaching; it was the duds "phoning it in." Although he had many good teachers, he recalled, "some were just not really paying attention, and I thought, 'I can do that job better than they can, and it's an important enough job to do well.'" Gary wasn't the first or last cocky teen to make this proclamation; he is, though, one of the handful who deliver on the threat.

At 55 and 3 decades into his career, Gary's middle age announces itself via his professorial white–gray Van Dyke, but then his blue eyes flash, revealing the rebellious teenager still inside. Conventional wisdom holds that elementary teachers love children and high school teachers love content. Yet Gary Anderson clearly loves teenagers as much as he loves books. And he adores books, reading 142 in one recent year alone.

There's lots of ways to meet Gary. For many Augusts, hundreds of young residents of Palatine, a suburb of Chicago, met him on the first day of English class at William Fremd High School. Across the country, more students meet him when assigned *Expository Writing: Discovering Your Voice*, a textbook he coauthored. Hundreds of teachers meet him at educational conferences; more meet him via his *What's Not Wrong?* blog. We first encountered him on Twitter, where he shares teaching ideas and book reviews.

He had somber news for us when we met him at a library near Palatine. Hurrying from the airport to our scheduled interview, we hadn't heard that two bombs had exploded at the Boston Marathon. Already, Gary knew that his plans for the next day, when we were to visit his classes, would have to take account of this new tragedy, close on the heels of the Newtown massacre.

This raised a topic we hadn't intended to cover that day: school security. In the months since Adam Lanza had blasted his way into Connecticut's Sandy Hook Elementary School to kill 26 children and 6 faculty and staff, the topic had embroiled the nation, with some debating whether or not to arm teachers. Over the years, Fremd had already made numerous changes in response to school shootings. After Columbine, a glass wall alongside the cafeteria was replaced with a solid one. Lockdown drills are common; the faculty has undergone live shooter simulations; classroom doors now lock when closed; and all students, staff, and visitors must wear a pass on a lanyard to get into and traverse the building. While Gary initially resisted the idea of being tagged like livestock, he came to terms with it, understanding the need for psychological safety. "In Maslow's hierarchy of needs, not getting shot is kind of the baseline," he says. "You can't do much else if you're worried about that. Our school and our district take that very, very seriously."[1]

Our conversation and those Gary would have the next day with his students are reminders of how much schools and teachers do to meet needs beyond academic ones—and reminders of how much of the outside world makes its way into the classroom, whether we lock the door behind us or not.

Gary is irreverent and strong-headed and can even, he admits, veer toward "self-righteous," particularly about school policies and teaching philosophies. He minced no words when it came to misguided education reforms, one-size-fits-all professional development, and overweening teachers. But asked about his school, he instantly mellowed. His Palatine students were "terrific," and Fremd, he repeated several times, was "a fine school."

Although when we visited he'd been there 26 years, Gary didn't start at Fremd. His first job after college was in Madrid, Iowa, a 15-minute hop down Route 17 from Boone. Madrid High had fewer than 200 enrolled students. Fremd has 2,400.

Gary became restless in the state where his grandfathers had mined coal and worked the railroad and his father had resettled after a military career. He was ready to follow his wife's career path out of Iowa. Still, he told us he "wouldn't trade those 5 years [at Madrid High] for anything. I knew everybody in town, and everybody knew me. It was so small that you could process students one at a time, and you would have the same kids even multiple years in a row. Everybody was an individual, but everybody was part of something larger, too." In sizeable-suburb Palatine, he kept the small-town Madrid attitude of teaching "one kid at a time."

By *kids*, Gary means adolescents. He's taught nothing but. It's not the age group most adults find especially delightful. But for Gary, the best thing about his work is that it's with teenagers, those bundles of contradictions. He noted, "Although some of them have been roughed up, high school students are for the most part pretty idealistic. They have a strong sense of how things should be. They hate being judged, but they are the most judgmental people in the world." His greatest joy is in helping his students "live up to their ideals, find their way to them."

The community is another source of Gary's job satisfaction. Palatine is a well-off town; its median family income, near $74,000, is roughly 40% above the national number.[2] Overall, Palatine parents support education strongly and are responsive if Gary calls home about a child's behavior or academics. Motorola, with operations in nearby Schaumburg, employs many Fremd parents as managers and engineers, including some from Korea and India "who have done well through education and value education for their kids, too." This fosters a high-powered academic environment that allows Gary to challenge his students—and himself—intellectually.

The full picture, however, is more complicated. From homeless children to multimillionaires' heirs, the student body runs the socioeconomic gamut. "The top and the bottom are a long ways apart," Gary explained, "and we have more at the top than we have at the bottom, but we've got everything." The Great Recession battered Palatine families on each rung of the income ladder, leaving some parents without time or energy to ensure homework got done. And Gary saw the recession further widen inequality there, as it had across the nation.

He wanted us to understand that it's not all rosy for his students, regardless of social class. "What some kids' lives are like is just unbelievable," he said with astonished admiration. "I don't know how they get through the day." Suburban kids, like their counterparts in urban and rural areas, can be affected by profound family financial, emotional, and health problems, even catastrophes. Sadly, over the years, Gary's seen too many parents with substance abuse problems. Often, "the kid is trying to do the right thing," self-parenting and avoiding substances, but sometimes "just gets sucked up into it." Other parents live in practiced denial about their teens' abuse and addiction problems. In fact, research has shown that children of affluence demonstrate high levels of substance use, anxiety, and depression, traced to profound pressure to achieve and isolation from parents.[3] For these students and others such as the children of couples who are divorcing, divorced, or good candidates for a split, school can provide a welcome distraction or escape—or added stress. When family dramas are weighing heavily on a child, Gary might cut that student some slack for a late assignment or a poor test grade, or recognize that the child needs more help than he can give, the kind the guidance counselor can provide.

* * *

In the morning, we drove to William Fremd, which had been plopped in a cornfield in 1963 and is now hemmed in by housing developments and retail strips. At a sign crowned with an image of the school's Viking mascot, we pulled into the vast parking lot fronting the building as hundreds of students hauling backpacks streamed inside.

At a security kiosk in the lobby, we were issued passes with our photos on them and waited for Gary, who had spent the morning in professional development meetings while we, and his students, had slept in and eaten breakfast. He greeted us wearing a polo shirt and khakis, the unofficial, unexciting uniform of America's male schoolteachers, though he'd jazzed it up with red-laced Nikes on his feet and pieces of flair on his lanyard.

It was time for Gary's first class, so we headed with him to beat his seniors to expository writing. Educators think they can tell much about a teacher just by his classroom setup. For high school teachers, who can't always personalize their rooms because they usually share them, this mostly means assessing desk arrangements. Are they in rows, suggesting an old-school approach (the teacher does lots of talking), clustered into tables (the students do lots of group work), or in a semicircle or U shape (everybody engages in lots of discussion)?

When we entered the room, its tablet-arm chairs were in a U shape. This configuration supported Gary's self-description as more "guide on the side" than "sage on the stage," language adopted from an influential piece by Alison King.[4] It's shorthand for a learning theory that swept American education in the late 20th century, just as Gary was starting his career. "Constructivism" put the student at the center, under the belief that information can be delivered by teachers through drill and lecture but that to acquire deep knowledge, students must actively make meaning through discussion and exploration.

Despite the day's late start, Gary's seniors moved into the room at the pace of cold maple syrup spreading across a plate. Many shambled in with eyes down, checking their smartphones for any social media activity they might have missed in the past few minutes. Every teacher in the United States today deals with the fact that teens turning off their phones feel they are committing a dereliction of duty comparable to that of an army sentinel's taking a snooze. The expected reward for constant vigilance is social relevance. When one boy slid into his seat, the girl next to him cheerily informed him without looking up from her phone, "You were blowing up on Twitter last night!"

To absorb his students in the work of class, Gary must briefly muffle social media's siren song, which thanks to the prevalence of smartphones can keep students entangled in family and peer dramas in class.[5] He accomplishes this most days by providing 10 to 15 minutes at the beginning of class for students to detach from their phones and to rediscover the printed page, reading books they've chosen or writing in response to prompts he's chosen. But this was no ordinary day, so after reviewing the agenda, he asked, "Does anyone have anything they want to talk about?"

They plunged in. A student brought up the marathon bombing, offering an estimate of the number of injured, prompting an argument about the facts and guesses at the bombers' identities. Gary asked how students found out about the event, and most had first heard about it online. They grappled awkwardly, like the media sources they'd been following, with the confusing swirl of speculation.

In every class, Gary introduced the topic gently; each held a very different discussion. He didn't push too far—this was just a chance to voice raw reactions—and his calm, nonjudgmental tone invited sharing. The more jaded seniors skated the surface; an earnest group of sophomores peeked under it, more reflective and analytical. A few students were critical of the media; others were optimistic that some good could come from the bad. Several expressed anger or frustration. When Gary suggested that Americans might be getting numb to acts of mass violence, one boy responded, "What else am I supposed to do? I can give blood, I can donate stuff, but I have to live my life."

Holding such a forum may sound more like the job of a guidance counselor than that of an English teacher, but it's a pragmatic move. When their strong emotional responses to real world events are articulated and reflected on, teens can clarify their values; when fear, anxiety, or anger are ignored, they can find it difficult to focus on academics.[6] Current events also provide opportunities for students to practice being critical consumers of media, as we saw Gary's students doing.

The purpose of his subject, as Gary sees it, is not just to prepare students to communicate effectively in the workplace. And the purpose of education broadly, he believes, is "to maximize the potential of each human being and to take society through its citizenry to the highest possible level." Fearful of appearing too lofty, he continued, "I don't want to get too cosmic or karmic here." Still, he wants to help his students become adults "who are informed and enlightened and actualized, and know what it means to be a part of something bigger than themselves, whether it's a family or a community or a nation or a world. And know how to contribute to that: to have the tools and the moral oomph, the moral imperative, to want to make things better." So at the end of one of the more insightful discussions of the Boston tragedy, he told the class with conviction, "I'm glad smart young people are thinking about these things."

Back in the first period, in expository writing, when Gary sensed the discussion of the bombings had run its course, he returned to the agenda. Knowing the routine, students dug into backpacks to unearth books and notebooks. Some began scribbling, answering the day's open-ended prompt Gary had written on the board. Others began reading.

Gary moved around the room, taking attendance and checking on students' progress with the titles they'd chosen. In the English classroom, there are few easier ways to personalize instruction than to allow student choice in reading, which has been shown to increase motivation and engagement.[7] Still, this can make teachers and parents nervous, fearing students will make poor choices. And the Common Core is shifting emphasis away from imaginative literature and student choice to close reading instruction using complex, Core-recommended nonfiction texts.[8] It is hard though to argue that a book of literary merit that lies unopened is a better book than an easy or weakly written one that is picked up and enjoyed. From our seats, we could see one boy with *The Catcher in the Rye* and another with *The Lord of the Flies*. Books from fantasy series (*The Lord of the Rings, The Hunger Games*) were popular, and though a few titles of dubious quality were in evidence, many were classics or otherwise challenging texts.

A couple of things came to mind watching 20-some-odd teenagers with their noses in books. The first was that American high school students don't read much anymore. The second was that these were spring semester seniors; they should have been slumping. Instead, we were surrounded by young people who appeared to be posing for one of the glossy "READ" posters that hang in libraries.

Critics of the education system like to point out that high school reading scores have remained stagnant over the past 40 years despite improvements at the lower levels.[9] Secondary English teachers, though, might be surprised they're not worse. After all, these lovers of literature know the dirty truth: Most students have no time or energy for reading—because they are each holding down the equivalent of one full-time job plus one second, part-time job consuming other media. On average, American teenagers spend roughly 60 hours a week on computers, TVs, and mobile devices and texting and talking on mobile phones.[10] According to the Kaiser Family Foundation, which collected these astounding statistics, teenagers still average 25 minutes a day of reading for pleasure, though often while at the same time watching TV or texting.

And the books assigned in English class? The Internet deserves blame here, too, for fewer students tackling Shakespeare, Homer, Austen, and Twain. Once upon a time, a panicked teen encountering *Macbeth* might hustle to the local bookseller to hunt down the CliffsNotes. Chances were that someone else in the class got there first. Today, even strong readers and responsible students are tempted by the proliferation of free online "study guides" at websites such as SparkNotes and Shmoop. These summarize and analyze virtually any text found in high school bookrooms, making it a breeze for students to fake it through discussions and quizzes.

So, the 10 class minutes Gary gives his students provide a chance to unplug, increasing an average teen's independent daily reading time by 40%. "If you want kids to read: opportunity, praise, choice," he told us. Opportunity is the prerequisite, and in a world in which unplugging seems impossible, reading has become a higher use of class time. Some teachers, administrators, and parents view devoting class time to reading as a waste of precious instructional minutes that could be better spent discussing a whole-class text, studying a grammar concept, or practicing a writing skill. With educators being urged to consider how they might "flip the classroom"–that is, think about what classwork tasks are better assigned as homework and vice versa– more may see value in carving reading time out of each week.[11] After all, some conversations can be had via discussion boards, grammar can be practiced using online quizzes, and writing exercises can completed at home and submitted for teacher review.

While his students took this brief break from multitasking, Gary did not. He used the time to step into the hallway to meet one-on-one with kids about papers they were drafting. In a sprinkling of well-funded districts, English teachers teach one fewer class, enabling them to meet with students in "writing conferences," which research has shown improves student writing in a way that written comments cannot. As budgets get squeezed even in wealthy areas, most teachers who believe in the value of conferences must build them into class time.

Gary took time this period for four individual meetings, each part of a longer-running conversation about the student's writing strengths and weaknesses. In each, he had concrete suggestions to supplement his written comments. In each, the tone was collaborative ("We've been working and succeeding in making your writing better") and supportive ("You didn't used to be able to do these things you are now doing").

With Gary out of the room, though visible in the doorway, overwhelmingly, students kept reading or moved on to the writing task. A few took the chance to quickly check phones, and two girls paused to reapply lip gloss. One gum chewer daydreamed before commencing a leisurely scroll on his phone, but while this pony wouldn't drink the water he'd been led to, he was an outlier. The others were lapping it up.

Because of the shortened schedule and time devoted to discussing the bombings, the period was near its end when Gary finished his last conference. With minutes to spare, he sought students to share what they'd written. A girl raised her hand. "I wrote about how society pressures us to fit as much as possible into a 24-hour day," she said. Asked to elaborate, she described the intense pressure she and her classmates feel to load their schedules with so many difficult classes that they "don't enjoy high school." And then, as if on anxious cue, the bell rang.

* * *

The level of trust Gary gives his students is the level of trust he'd like to see teachers get, especially highly capable ones. Working to reach children one at a time, he's frustrated that teachers are treated as one indistinguishable mass, regardless of training, experience, or reputation. When it comes to what is called professional development, such as that which the Fremd faculty attended that morning, Gary, like many of his counterparts across the nation, can sometimes become more bitter than better.

Professional development, or PD, is meant to build on teachers' existing knowledge and skills. Often taking place after school or during summer, the training each state requires is of a different amount and type, and districts often overlay their own requirements. Rapidly changing technology, a diversifying student population, an ever-shifting legal landscape, and revolving curricula mean teachers can always benefit from this kind of update.

Yet teachers can complain that what they usually get served at school or district-led PD sessions is a big, sloppy helping of the Flavor of the Month.[12] For a while, maybe just a year, it's all about reaching individual students through differentiation—nothing is more important! The next year it's all about interdisciplinary connections, and differentiation goes out the window. Then suddenly, it's all about metacognition, and then that interdisciplinary thing again. And so it goes.

Gary is one of these teachers with a jaundiced eye toward PD efforts. "The priorities from 5 years ago, they're gone. The priorities from 2 years ago are gone," he told us. While some elements of prior initiatives remain, much is abandoned as the current focus, sometimes complementary to and sometimes contradictory of earlier initiatives, is pushed. Lately there'd been a grinding consistency, driven by the pressure to stoke standardized test scores. "For the past 5 years," it seemed to Gary, "100% of our on-site professional development has been about assessment." As in many districts, teachers were being taught how to preassess students, assess them, and assess them again, to get these students ready . . . to be assessed.

On an anecdotal basis, teachers could tell you how the training they received on an online grading system has opened communication with parents. On a qualitative basis, they could tell you whether or not a workshop on questioning techniques has deepened class discussions. But as the overarching goal of many districts has become improving test scores, quantitative measures have become the only measures given much merit. The obsession with test data started, Gary believes, with No Child Left Behind. Since then, "it seems like some people can't understand what progress looks like unless it's in a numerical, maybe even color-coded, chart. If you tell somebody a story, it may be true that it really happened, but where's the proof? But if you give them a data chart with percent signs and decimal points in it, even if it's based on hallucination, they'll say, 'Oh, you can clearly see the progress here!'"

Gary wryly applied a scatological metaphor: There's too much worry about what comes out the end, not what goes in the front. Yet what teachers want, he said, is to keep getting better at motivating students and designing their lessons.

At the same time, the data crunching didn't seem to him to be pushing the needle it was meant to push. "There is no evidence that any of it makes a difference. We've plowed into it so much time, energy, and resources, and our test scores, which are what it's really aimed at, have pretty much re-mained flat. Our scores are not bad, they are not even close to bad, but they haven't changed."

What Gary has found especially effective is collaborating with teach-ers in other districts and states. A few years ago, dispirited by the amount of time he was spending not talking about what good teaching looks like, the technophile turned to social media to connect with educators elsewhere. Since then, he's been energized, sharing ideas with English teachers across the country and in turn learning from them about methods that work. As are more and more teachers, Gary is in effect participating in a kind of bottom-up "shadow" program that addresses the weaknesses of top-down systems of professional development.

When we stopped into the English department office between bells so Gary could drop off one set of class materials and pick up another, we couldn't help noticing that the desks of the 28 members of the department were wedged into a single, pretty small room. And they must be good at sharing, because each teacher works at a 3-by-5-foot desk facing another teacher. Student cars in the parking lot had more space. Gary, though, was surprisingly upbeat about it. His colleagues get along well, and he credited some of that collegiality to their close quarters. Here, Fremd teachers continue developing professionally through that low-tech collaboration of talking.

We were off to two consecutive sections of accelerated sophomore Eng-lish for more advanced 10th-grade readers and writers. After the Boston dis-cussion and independent reading, the class would analyze the whole-class book they were studying, Amy Tan's *The Joy Luck Club*. First, though, Gary projected the blog he maintains for his classes on the social network site Ning, revealing where the blog's newest readers ("their fans") were located. Real audiences for their work motivate students to write, and Gary likes to remind his that people around the world are reading their book reviews and other pieces. They chuckled when he described a link he'd posted to a free audio book site as "highly clickable." They really seemed to like him, which matters. He's their number one fan, the primary audience for their work. Yet having that larger audience was clearly inspiring; here was a teacher turning his students' propensity to use social media to his advantage, understanding that it can be an attraction to, not just a distraction from, academic pursuits.

As the class dug into *The Joy Luck Club*, discussion energetically swung from issues of basic comprehension to deep analysis and back. They shared insights about lost children, a key motif, and Gary affirmed their thinking or prodded for more. Students of both genders seemed comfortable showing smarts and revealing confusion, and when the bell rang and Gary said, "We need a whole hour for this class today," several yelled, "Yes!"

Later in the day, two classes of less excited seniors were provided more structure for the challenge of Chaucer: a packet of comprehension questions about "The Wife of Bath's Tale" that Gary took them through methodically.

Although hardly relishing the rhymes thrown down by the granddaddy of English literature 6 centuries ago, they stuck with it, a smattering offering up answers and the rest scribbling them down.

With all the comings and goings during the school day–rushing from meeting to class to study hall to class to class to lunch to class to class, there wasn't time for Gary to take a 2-minute break, much less sit down and grade or plan the next day's classes. Paper and test grading would get done at home. For a full load of five classes, that could conceivably total 300 grading hours a year–equivalent to a summer break.

The next year would be Gary's last at Fremd. When a recent contract had been reached between the teachers and District 211, he told us, he realized that he was being incentivized to retire. Ironically, given the difficulties schools face in retaining newer teachers and improving overall teacher quality, Gary was being nudged off the top of the pay scale so a new teacher could be slotted in at the bottom. Only in his 50s, with children still to put through college and as much enthusiasm for teaching as ever, Gary didn't expect to stop working. He'd be prohibited from teaching in an Illinois public school once his pension payments started, he told us, so he might seek work at an independent school, maybe a middle school, which is when too many kids stop reading. Those would be the children to benefit from a veteran in their classroom who loves them as much as he loves books.

Questions for Discussion

- What responsibility do teachers have to keep their students safe or to provide them with a sense of safety?
- How are the challenges faced by teachers in affluent schools similar to and unique from those faced in less affluent ones?
- Can teachers turn social media and other time-consuming technologies from a distraction from academic work to an invitation to it?
- In the effort to develop lifelong readers, how important is it to provide students with time to read and choice in books? What other factors are key?
- How can teachers take more active roles in their professional development?

Suggestions for Further Reading

Asselin, M., and Moayeri, M. "The Participatory Classroom: Web 2.0 in the Classroom." *Literacy Learning: The Middle Years,* 19 (June 2011): i–vii.

Cowan, K. C., and Rossen, E. "Responding to the Unthinkable: School Crisis Response and Recovery." *Phi Delta Kappan,* 95, no. 4 (2013–2014): 8–12.

Martin, L. E., Kragler, S., Quatroche, D. J., and Bauserman, K. L. *Handbook of Professional Development in Education: Successful Models and Practices, PreK–12* (Guilford Press, 2014).

Moss, B., and Young, T. *Creating Lifelong Readers Through Independent Reading* (International Reading Association, 2010).

Tobias, S., and Duffy, T. M. *Constructivist Instruction: Success or Failure?* (Routledge, 2009).

conclusion

Over one mind-opening year, we met nine of America's teachers. At the end of the school days on which we observed them, we were exhausted. At the end of each of our interviews, we were in equal measure inspired. And we were inspired, even though what they shared about the challenging lives of some students could be dispiriting. To hear how these teachers talked about the children who are their students—with love, admiration, and hope—was, though, uplifting. Most powerful of all was to see those children in the classroom learning, engaged with their teachers, and having worlds opened to them at each turn.

In their interviews, the 9 were far more inclined to share their pleasures than their pains. Yet their frustrations were real, reflecting larger public concerns about trends in society and education, and one of them has since left the classroom.

Schooled's teachers see their missions in broad terms. Along with traditional academics, these teachers seek to provide students with social skills, problem-solving skills, the ability to express themselves and be creative, and insight into their strengths and how to use them in lifelong pursuits. They believe they can achieve these ambitious goals when they are allowed as professionals to produce motivation and learning based on students' individual needs, developmental stages, and cultural and community values.

Many feel their mission is threatened by harmful social and economic trends and by elements of modern education reform. Yet the silver lining of working in this crucible is the crystallization of what is truly important, what is at the heart of teaching well—which teachers might not, under less challenging circumstances, have understood as clearly. It is time for this well of understanding to be tapped.

* * *

When we set ourselves the task of writing about American teachers, our goal was not simply to celebrate them. It was to listen and to give a few of them a voice, a voice that was being silenced in an ever-louder national debate about education. Here is some of what we heard:

- **Educational reforms are needed and some positive changes are under way.** Teachers are rejoicing at the establishment of programs addressing some of the social issues inhibiting children's ability to learn. One example is school breakfast programs such as those in St. Paul and Colorado Springs, where we witnessed students eating healthy meals at the start of the day. Without the national focus on STEM, the Center for Sustainable Solutions, in which Lisa Myrick works, would not exist; she is optimistic about how the investment will pay off in sustainable, sociopositive careers for her students. Without the STEM push, there would also likely be no flight simulator lab at Jack Swigert; Robert Lewis is excited that his middle schoolers have access to this technology.

- **Unfortunately, many reforms are hurting rather than helping students.** Topping the list is the boom in standardized testing and the mounting focus on test results. *Schooled's* teachers were concerned about the impact on students of testing; many saw heightened stress and dampened motivation among their students who are frequently facing high-stakes tests. The experience of teachers such as Lindsey McClintock demonstrated how a fixation on test results—including their factoring into teacher evaluation and pay—can narrow the curriculum, reducing the time students are working on anything other than math or reading skills.

- **These top-down reforms too often treat all schools, teachers, and students the same way.** When the curriculum narrows, students whose talents lie in the arts or whose disabilities mean that they cannot show what they know via traditional tests are among those who suffer. Gifted students can find it harder to stretch when much instruction is test preparation. Some teachers see community values threatened by federal directives; to preserve funding, Pine Ridge Reservation schools must adopt the Common Core though Native language and culture lessons are at that community's core. And though *Schooled's* teachers were eager to develop, several saw professional development efforts as flawed when they treat teachers the same way regardless of subject area or experience level. A failure to individualize instruction for students is motivating some parents to abandon the system altogether and homeschool.

- **Austerity is having a detrimental impact on teaching and learning.** The failure to fully restore school funding cut during the recession is making it more difficult to teach and learn. Colorado Springs' furlough days may be the most obvious manifestation of this—teachers don't teach and children don't learn when kept out of school. The most deleterious effects of budget cuts, however, likely result from increased class sizes, which we witnessed at several schools. Among other things, larger classes increase teachers' grading loads at night and decrease the attention they can give each student during the day.

- **At the same time that teachers are asked to do too much, they are asked to do too little.** Teachers are taking on additional responsibilities once handled by districts, communities, and families, including fundraising and paying for supplies, even buying food for students. Budget cuts and reforms have teachers doing work wasteful of their training and talent. Some, such as Ulla Tervo-Desnick, can feel like data entry clerks; others, such as Lindsey McClintock, find themselves used as babysitters and traffic wardens. Although we saw some, including Lisa Myrick and Gary Anderson, exercising flexibility, standardized curriculum and scripted lessons are preventing other teachers from improving and innovating.

- **Teachers feel the weight of public perception.** Whether working in a traditional public, charter, or independent school; tenured or not; new or veteran; schoolteacher or homeschooler; first-grade or AP teacher, *Schooled*'s teachers overwhelmingly feel that the public undervalues their work. Teachers find this public image discouraging given their commitment, educational level and expertise, and workload. More than one thought that its practitioners, male and female, suffer from teaching being seen dismissively as women's work.

- **Reform efforts can be based on a serious misreading of teachers' motivations.** Many modern reform efforts are geared toward teacher accountability; this presumes that teachers don't feel intrinsically accountable for their students' success and well-being. *Schooled*'s teachers, however, felt answerable to their students in profound ways. They are personally, culturally, even spiritually bound to their communities, as Glorianna Under Baggage, Ann Marie Donnelly, and Robert Lewis perhaps illustrated best. Merit pay is predicated on the notion that teachers will produce more if paid for "performance." Our teachers, however, aren't motivated this way. Even teachers who would likely "win out" in a merit-pay system saw such systems as counterproductive. This isn't to say that teachers don't want to be paid well. In many cases, our teachers could essentially "afford" to teach because they were not the only or highest-paid breadwinners in their families.

- **Teachers are pushing when they can, not as much *against* anything as *for* something.** Some are doing this in dramatic ways, as Stacey Harrell did in cofounding a charter school with a mission she believed in. More are doing this in myriad, quieter ways, stealing minutes here and there to promote the learning they believe in, or pursuing their own "shadow" professional development, as we saw Gary Anderson do. Some are defying directives in small acts of civil disobedience. While teachers feel they are being held accountable for much outside their control, they are holding themselves accountable to use the control they do have to hold on to their ideals.

* * *

Like many others in the field, *Schooled*'s teachers know that their expertise stems not just from their mastery of modern pedagogy but also from their deep knowledge of their particular communities and students. The knowledge that teachers acquire, either by being members of a community or by gradually learning more about their students' lives and challenges, helps them become better teachers. So does having the confidence to use the pedagogical values they learned in training and in practice in crafting their lessons. Knowing that reading choice can help students unplug, knowing that a passive student may not be recalcitrant but tired from sleeping on the floor the night before, knowing that what special-needs children need most is the gift of time to learn and relearn, teachers can and do continue to teach in the ways they believe are best.

For teachers to stay motivated and committed to their educational ideals, it is critical that they find and use their individual voices and collective voice. This may mean speaking up in faculty meetings, sharing concerns about policy changes, or brainstorming how to achieve school goals threatened by outside directives. This may mean advocating within or on behalf of their union for the compensation and conditions that enable them to teach effectively. This may mean making their views known to policymakers at district- and state-level board of education meetings. This may mean using traditional and social media to make visible to taxpayers, parents, and policymakers the positive work going on in classrooms that they wish to preserve. The more teachers speak up, the more they share their stories of what it means to teach today, the more they motivate each other to do the same. The greater the chance they then have of moving off the sidelines to become key voices in the policy conversations about education. With the experience and expertise of teachers at the center of a stronger, smarter national commitment to better educating our children, this age of change can be a phenomenal one.

notes

Introduction

1. Trevor Tompson, Jennifer Benz, and Jennifer Agiesta, *Parents' Attitudes About the Quality of Education in the United States*, The Associated Press–NORC Center for Public Affairs Research, August 2013, http:// www.apnorc.org/PDFs/Parent%20Attitudes/AP_NORC_Parents%20 Attitudes%20on%20the%20Quality%20of%20Education%20in%20the%20 US_FINAL_2.pdf

2. Karen J. DeAngelis and Jennifer B. Presley, "Toward a More Nuanced Understanding of New Teacher Attrition," *Education and Urban Society,* 43 (2011): 598–626. Another study found that 7% of the teaching work force leaves the profession each year. Dan Goldhaber and James Cowan, "Excavating the Teacher Pipeline: Teacher Preparation Programs and Teacher Attrition," *Journal of Teacher Education,* 65 (2014): 449–462.

3. It has been estimated that 3.5 million public school teachers, and 4.2 million teachers in all types of schools, would retire from 2009 to 2020. Daniel Aaronson and Katherine Meckel, "How Will Baby Boomer Retirements Affect Teacher Labor Markets?" *Economic Perspectives,* Federal Reserve Bank of Chicago (4Q/2009): 2–15.

4. Lis Power, Hilary Tone, and Jessica Torres, "Report: Only 9 Percent of Guests Discussing Education on Evening Cable News Were Educators," *Media Matters,* November 20, 2014, http://mediamatters.org/research/2014/11/20/ report-only-9-percent-of-guests-discussing-educ/201659

5. The data show that 6.2 million adults are on schools' staff and 55 million students are enrolled in K–12. National Center for Education Statistics (NCES), "Table 92. Staff Employed in Public Elementary and Secondary School Systems, by Type of Assignment: Selected Years, 1949– 1950 Through Fall 2010," *Digest of Education Statistics,* 2012, http://nces. ed.gov/programs/digest/d12/tables/dt12_092.asp

6. Emily Feistritzer, *Profile of Teachers in the U.S. 2011* (Washington, DC: National Center for Education Information, 2011), http://www.edweek.org/ media/pot2011final-blog.pdf

7. Feistritzer, *Profile of Teachers.*

8. National Center for Education Statistics, "Table 216.20. Number and Enrollment of Public Elementary and Secondary Schools, by School Level,

Type, and Charter and Magnet Status: Selected Years, 1990–1991 Through 2011–2012," *Digest of Education Statistics*, 2012.

9. G. Kena, S. Aud, F. Johnson, X. Wang, J. Zhang, A. Rathbun, S. Wilkinson-Flicker, and P. Kristapovich, *The Condition of Education 2014* (NCES 2014-083) (Washington, DC: U.S. Department of Education, National Center for Education Statistics, 2014), http://nces.ed.gov/pubsearch

10. Feistritzer, *Profile of Teachers.*

11. Feistritzer, *Profile of Teachers.*

12. National Center for Education Statistics (NCES), *Digest of Education Statistics*, http://nces.ed.gov/pubs2013/2013028/tables/table_07.asp

13. Scholastic and the Bill and Melinda Gates Foundation, *Primary Sources: 2012; America's Teachers on the Teaching Profession*, http://www.scholastic.com/primarysources/pdfs/Gates2012_full.pdf

14. Ulrich Boser and Chelsea Straus, *Mid- and Late-Career Teachers Struggle with Paltry Incomes*, Center for American Progress, July 23, 2014, http://cdn.americanprogress.org/wp-content/uploads/2014/07/teachersalaries-brief.pdf

15. Dana Markow and Andrea Pieters, *Teachers, Parents, and the Economy: A Survey of Teachers, Parents, and Students*, The MetLife Survey of the American Teacher, March 2012, http://files.eric.ed.gov/fulltext/ED530021.pdf

16. Markow and Pieters, *Teachers, Parents, and the Economy.*

17. See Dana Goldstein, *The Teacher Wars: A History of America's Most Embattled Profession* (New York: Doubleday, 2014).

18. Steve Suitts, Nasheed Sabree, and Katherine Dunn, *A New Majority: Low Income Students in the South and Nation*, Southern Education Foundation, October 2013, http://www.southerneducation.org/Our-Strategies/Research-and-Publications/New-Majority-Diverse-Majority-Report-Series/A-New-Majority-Low-Income-Students-in-the-South-s.aspx

19. Richard M. Ingersoll, *Who Controls Teachers' Work? Power and Accountability in America's Schools* (Cambridge, MA: Harvard University Press, 2003), 148–149.

20. Since 2003, 8th-grade scores have risen 5 points in reading and 7 points in math (on a 500-point scale). National Center for Education Statistics, *The Nation's Report Card: A First Look: 2013; Mathematics and Reading* (NCES 2014-451) (Washington, DC: Institute of Education Sciences, U.S. Department of Education, 2013).

Chapter 1

1. U.S. Department of Education, Office of Innovation and Improvement, *Creating Successful Magnet Schools Programs* (Washington, DC: U.S. Department of Education, 2004); Adam Gamoran, "Student Achievement in Public Magnet, Public Comprehensive, and Private City High Schools," *Educational Evaluation and Policy Analysis*, 18, no. 1 (1996): 1–18.

2. EXPO Elementary School, Saint Paul Public Schools, http://expo.spps.org/

3. A 2014 agreement reached between the St. Paul Public Schools and the teachers union included some class-size reductions. Tim Post, "Pay Raise, Smaller Class Sizes Included in St. Paul Teachers Contract Agreement," Minnesota Public Radio, February 24, 2014, http://www.mprnews.org/story/2014/02/24/st-paul-teachers-union-district-agreement; see also Bruce J. Biddle and David C. Berliner, "Small Class Size and Its Effects," *Educational Leadership*, 59, no. 5 (2002): 12–23.

4. "Hunger-Free Minnesota Announces Initiative to Increase Participation in School Breakfast Program: Eating School Breakfast Improves Academic Performance," PRWEB, September 6, 2012, http://www.prweb.com/releases/2012/9/prweb9868405.htm; J. Michael Murphy, "Breakfast and Learning: An Updated Review," *Current Nutrition & Food Science*, 3, no. 1 (2007): 3–36.

5. Responsive Classroom, Northeast Foundation for Children, http://www.responsiveclassroom.org/; Sara E. Rimm-Kaufman and Yu-Jen I. Chiu, "Promoting Social and Academic Competence in the Classroom: An Intervention Study Examining the Contribution of the Responsive Classroom Approach," *Psychology in the Schools*, 4, no. 4 (2007): 397–413.

6. Sara E. Rimm-Kaufman, R.A.A. Larsen, A.E. Baroody, T.W. Curby, M. Ko, J.B. Thomas, E.G. Meritt, T. Abry, & J. DeCoster. "Efficacy of the Responsive Classroom Approach: Results from a 3-Year, Longitudinal Randomized Controlled Trial," *American Educational Research Journal*, 51, no. 3 (2014): 567–603.

7. Pasi Sahlberg, *Finnish Lessons: What Can the World Learn from Educational Change in Finland?* (New York: Teacher's College Press, 2011), 63–65.

8. Sahlberg, *Finnish Lessons*, 63–65.

9. "Testing Information," Minnesota Department of Education, http://education.state.mn.us/mde/justparent/testreq/index.html

10. Saint Paul Public Schools Data Center, Saint Paul Public Schools, http://datacenter.spps.org/

11. Daarel Burnette, "Magnet Schools Lose Pull," *StarTribune*, April 12, 2011, http://www.startribune.com/local/stpaul/119667429.html

Chapter 2

1. Ben Casselman, "Race Gap Narrows in College Enrollment, but Not in Graduation," *Five Thirty Eight Economics*, April 30, 2014, http://fivethirtyeight.com/features/race-gap-narrows-in-college-enrollment-but-not-in-graduation/

2. Nicole Leinbach-Reyhle, "Teachers Spend Their Own Money on Back to School Supplies," *Forbes.com*, August 19, 2014.

3. www.donorschoose.org

4. Michael Leachman and Chris Mai, "Most States Funding Schools Less Than Before the Recession," Center on Budget and Policy Priorities, May 20, 2014, http://www.cbpp.org/cms/index.cfm?fa=view&id=4213

5. Connecticut State Department of Education, Bureau of Grants Management, 2013–14 Net Current Expenditures (NCE) per Pupil (NCEP) and 2014–2015 Special Education Excess Cost Grant, February 2015, http://www.sde.ct.gov/sde/lib/sde/PDF/dgm/report1/basiccon.pdf

6. Bruce D. Baker, *Private Schooling in the U.S.: Expenditures, Supply, and Policy Implications* (East Lansing, MI: The Great Lakes Center for Education Research & Practice, August 2009).

7. D. Kalogrides, S. Loeb, and T. Beteille, "Systematic Sorting: Teacher Characteristics and Class Assignments," *Sociology of Education,* 86 (2012): 103–123.

8. Figures for 2010–2011. National Center for Education Statistics (December 2013), *Digest of Education Statistics, 2012,* http://nces.ed.gov/pubs2014/2014015.pdf

9. Linda Darling-Hammond, "Reforming Teacher Preparation and Licensing: Debating the Evidence," *Teachers College Record,* 102 (2000): 28–56; Dale Ballou and Michael Podgursky, "Reforming Teacher Preparation and Licensing: What Is the Evidence?" *Teachers College Record,* 102 (2000): 5–27; Douglas N. Harris and Tim R. Sass, "Teacher Training, Teacher Quality, and Student Achievement," *Journal of Public Economics,* 95 (2000): 798–812.

10. The average Catholic school student–teacher ratio nationally is reported at 13:1 (compared with 15:1 in public schools). Cathedral is also an outlier from its Catholic peers in having mostly racial minority group members enrolled; the national average in Catholic schools is 20%. Dale McDonald and Margaret M. Schultz, *United States Catholic Elementary and Secondary Schools 2013–2014: The Annual Statistical Report on Schools, Enrollment, and Staffing,* National Catholic Education Association, 2014; National Center for Education Statistics (December 2013), Table 76. Public and Private Elementary and Secondary Teachers, Enrollment, and Pupil/Teacher Ratios: Selected Years, Fall 1955 through Fall 2012, *Digest of Education Statistics 2012,* http://nces.ed.gov/pubs2014/2014015.pdf

11. Scholastic and Bill and Melinda Gates Foundation, *Primary Sources: America's Teachers on Teaching in an Era of Change,* 3rd ed., 2014, http://www.scholastic.com/primarysources/PrimarySources3rdEditionWithAppendix.pdf

12. McDonald and Schultz, *United States Catholic Elementary and Secondary Schools.*

Chapter 3

1. Michael B. Berkman and Eric Plutzer, "Defeating Creationism in the Courtroom, but Not in the Classroom," *Science,* 331 (2011): 404–405.

2. Leah Todd, "Wyoming Blocks New Science Standards," *Caspar Star Tribune,* March 14, 2014, http://trib.com/news/local/education/wyoming-first-state-to-block-new-science-standards/article_5d0ec624-6b50-5354-b015-ca2f5f7d7efe.html

3. Gilbert High, *ProPublica,* http://projects.propublica.org/schools/schools/450270000726

4. Rachael Gabriel, Jeni Peiria Day, and Richard Allington, "Exemplary Teacher Voices on Their Own Development," *Kappan*, May 2011, 37–41.

5. Demetra Kalogrides, Susanna Loeb, and Tara Beteille, "Systematic Sorting: Teacher Characteristics and Class Assignments," *Sociology of Education*, 86 (2012): 103–123.

6. NASDAQ GlobeNewswire, *Education Technology and the Smart Classroom Market Report: Forecasts and Analysis 2013–2018*, November 13, 2013, http://globenewswire.com/news-release/2013/11/13/589556/10057819/en/ Education-Technology-and-the-Smart-Classroom-Market-Report-Forecasts- and-Analysis-2013-2018.html#sthash.dR4u9nEY.dpuf

7. Peter Dolton and Oscar Marcenaro-Gutierrez, *Varkey GEMS Foundation Global Teacher Status Index*, October 2013, https://www.varkeygemsfoundation. org/sites/default/files/documents/2013GlobalTeacherStatusIndex.pdf

8. Richard Ingersoll and Elizabeth Merrill, "The Status of Teaching as a Profession," in *Schools and Society: A Sociological Approach to Education*, ed. J. Ballantine and J. Spade, 4th ed. (Thousand Oaks, CA: Pine Forge Press/ Sage, 2011), 185–189.

9. Sam Ro, "What Teacher Pay Looks Like in the Rest of the World," *Business Insider*, July 18, 2013, http://www.businessinsider.com/countries- where-teachers-get-paid-more-2013-7

10. Ludger Woessmann, "Cross-Country Evidence on Teacher Performance Pay," *Economics of Education Review*, 30 (2011): 404–418; Michael Podgursky and Matthew G. Springer, "Credentials Versus Performance: Review of the Teacher Performance Pay Research," *Peabody Journal of Education*, 82 (2007): 551–573.

11. Cynthia Roldan, "Teacher Evaluation Bill Stalls in S.C. House Subcommittee," *The Post and Courier*, February 18, 2014, http://www. postandcourier.com/article/20140218/PC1603/140219325

12. Matthew G. Springer et al., *Teacher Pay for Performance: Experimental Evidence from the Project on Incentives in Teaching* (Nashville, TN: National Center on Performance Incentives at Vanderbilt University, September 21, 2010), https://my.vanderbilt.edu/performanceincentives/research/point-ex- periment/; see also Thomas S. Dee and Benjamin J. Keys, "Does Merit Pay Reward Good Teachers? Evidence from a Randomized Experiment," *Journal of Policy Analysis and Management*, 23 (2004): 471–488, which shows relatively minor improvements in math achievement.

13. Springer et al., *Teacher Pay for Performance.*

14. Gary W. Ritter, Joshua H. Barnett, and Nathan C. Jensen, "Making Sense of the Merit Pay Debate: A Synthesis of the Evidence" (paper presented at the Association for Education Finance and Policy 39th Annual Conference, San Antonio, TX, March 13, 2014), http://www.aefpweb.org/ sites/default/files/webform/39th/AEFP%20Merit%20Pay%20Review%20 -%20Ritter%20Barnett%20Jensen.pdf

15. "Scientist–Clinical Research, Median Salary," Salary.com, accessed November 4, 2014, http://swz.salary.com/salarywizard/Scientist-Clinical-

Research-Salary-Details-Columbia-SC.aspx?&hdcbxbonuse=off&isshowpie
chart=false&isshowjobchart=false&isshowsalarydetailcharts=true&isshowne
xtsteps=true&isshowcompanyfct=true&isshowaboutyou=true

Chapter 4

1. Lynn S. Fuchs, Douglas Fuchs, and Andrea M. Capizzi, "Identifying
Appropriate Test Accommodations for Students with Learning Disabilities,"
Focus on Exceptional Children, 37 (2005): 1–8.

2. This movement has been spearheaded at the Rhode Island School of
Design. www.stemtosteam.org.

3. J. Randy McGinnis, "Teaching Science to Learners with Special Needs,"
Theory into Practice, 52 (2013): 43–50.

4. Colorado Department of Education, CSAP/TCAP–Data and Results,
2014, http://www.cde.state.co.us/assessment/coassess-dataandresults

5. Martell L. Teasley, "Absenteeism and Truancy: Risk, Protection, and
Best Practice Implications for School Social Workers," *Children and Schools*, 26
(2004): 117–128; Kathleen L. Lane, Erik W. Carter, Melinda R. Pierson, and
Barbara C. Glaeser, "Academic, Social, and Behavioral Characteristics of
High School Students with Emotional Disturbances or Learning Disabilities,"
Journal of Emotional and Behavioral Disorders, 14 (2006): 108–117.

6. Steven Glazerman and Allison Seifullah, *An Evaluation of the Teacher
Advancement Program (TAP) in Chicago: Year Two Impact Report* (Princeton, NJ:
Mathematica Policy Research, 2010); Lewis Solmon, Todd White, Donna
Cohen, and Deborah Woo, *The Effectiveness of the Teacher Advancement Program*,
National Institute for Excellence in Teaching, 2007, http://talentedteachers.
com/pubs/effective_tap07_full.pdf

7. John Nunnery, Leslie Kaplan, William A. Owings, and S. Pribesh,
"The Effects of Troops to Teachers on Student Achievement: One State's
Study," *NASSP Bulletin*, February 3, 2010, http://www.dantes.doded.mil/
content/Owens_Study.pdf#zoom=100

8. U.S. Department of Education, Office of Postsecondary Education,
*Preparing and Credentialing the Nation's Teachers: The Secretary's Ninth Report
on Teacher Quality* (Washington, DC: U.S. Department of Education, 2013),
https://title2.ed.gov/TitleIIReport13.pdf

9. U.S. Department of Education, *Preparing and Credentialing*.

10. C. Emily Feistritzer, *Profile of Teachers in the U.S. 2011* (Washington,
DC: National Center for Education Information, 2011), http://www.edweek.
org/media/pot2011final-blog.pdf

11. Tim R. Sass, "Licensure and Worker Quality: A Comparison of
Alternative Routes to Teaching," *Ms.*, April 14, 2014, http://www2.gsu.
edu/~tsass/pdfs/Alternative%20Certification%20and%20Teacher%20
Quality%2013.pdf

12. Feistritzer, *Profile of Teachers*.

13. Morgaen L. Donaldson and Susan Moore Johnson, "TFA Teachers:
How Long Do They Teach? Why Do They Leave?" *Education Week*,

October 4, 2011, accessed November 14, 2014, http://www.edweek.org/ew/articles/2011/10/04/kappan_donaldson.html; Linda Darling-Hammond, Deborah J. Holtzman, Su Jin Gatlin, and Julian Vasquez Heilig, "Does Teacher Preparation Matter? Evidence About Teacher Certification, Teach for America, and Teacher Effectiveness," *Education Policy Analysis Archives*, 13 (2005), http://epaa.asu.edu/epaa/v13n42/

14. "Jack Swigert Aerospace Academy," GreatSchools, accessed November 14, 2014, http://www.greatschools.org/colorado/colorado-springs/4159-Jack-Swigert-Aerospace-Academy/

15. Ana Villegas and Jacqueline Irvine, "Diversifying the Teaching Force: An Examination of Major Arguments," *Urban Review*, 42 (2010): 175–192.

Chapter 5

1. Amber Noel, Patrick Stark, and Jeremey Redford, *Parent and Family Involvement in Education, from the National Household Education Surveys Program of 2012* (NCES 2013-028) (Washington, DC: National Center for Education Statistics, Institute of Education Sciences, U.S. Department of Education, 2013), http://nces.ed.gov/pubsearch; U.S. Department of Education, Institute of Education Sciences. *Digest of Education Statistics, 2012*, http://nces.ed.gov/programs/digest/d12/tables/dt12_040.asp

2. Joseph Murphy, *Home schooling in America: Capturing and Assessing the Movement* (New York: Sage, 2012): 79–80.

3. U.S. Department of Education, Institute of Education Sciences, *Digest of Education Statistics, 2012*, http://nces.ed.gov/pubs2013/2013028.pdf

4. A third option is an "alternative assessment" agreed upon by superintendent and parent. http://www.cheohome.org/get-started/year-end-evaluations/

5. Douglas Wilson, *The Case for Classical Christian Education* (Wheaton, IL: Crossway, 2003). See also www.classicalconversations.com

6. Murphy, *Homeschooling in America*, 16–20.

7. Mitchell Stevens, *Kingdom of Children: Culture and Controversy in the Home schooling Movement* (Princeton: Princeton University Press, 2001), 85.

8. Joseph Murphy, "The Social and Educational Outcomes of Home schooling," *Sociological Spectrum*, 34 (2014): 244–272.

9. Gene W. Gloeckner and Paul Jones, "Reflections on a Decade of Changes in Home schooling and the Home schooled into Higher Education," *Peabody Journal of Education*, 88 (2013): 309–323; M. Saunders, "Previously Home schooled College Freshmen: Their First Year Experiences and Persistence Rates," *Journal of College Student Retention*, 11 (2010): 77–100.

10. John Wesley Taylor V, "Self-Concept in Home-Schooling Children," *Home School Researcher*, 2 (1986): 1–3, cited in Murphy, *Home schooling in America*, 145–151.

11. Sharon Green-Hennessy, "Home schooled Adolescents in the United States: Developmental Outcomes," *Journal of Adolescence*, 37 (2014): 441–449.

12. Michael W. Apple, "Away with All the Teachers: The Cultural Politics of Home schooling," in *Home Schooling in Full View: A Reader*, ed. Bruce S. Cooper (Greenwich, CT: Information Age, 2005), 75–95.

Chapter 6

1. Luci Scott, "Schools Grapple with Substitute-Teacher Shortage," *AZ Central: 12 News and The Arizona Republic*, April 22, 2014, http://www.azcentral.com/story/news/local/chandler/2014/04/22/schools-grapple-substitute-teacher-shortage/7993625/; "Substitute Teacher, K–12 Salary (United States)," Payscale, accessed November 4, 2014, http://www.payscale.com/research/US/Job=Substitute_Teacher,_K-12/Hourly_Rate

2. Charlotte Danielson, *Enhancing Professional Practice: A Framework for Teaching* (Alexandria, VA: Association for Supervision and Curriculum Development, 1996).

3. An editorial from *The Los Angeles Times* summarizes some of these concerns. "Common Core Learning Curve," *The Los Angeles Times*, March 14, 2014, http://articles.latimes.com/2014/mar/14/opinion/la-ed-common-core-two-20140314

4. Xitao Fan and Michael Chen, "Parental Involvement and Students' Academic Achievement: A Meta-analysis," *Educational Psychology Review*, 13 (2001): 1–21; Kathleen Cotton and Karen Reed Wikelund, "Parent Involvement in Education," Education Northwest, School Improvement Research Series, May 1989, http://educationnorthwest.org/sites/default/files/parent-involvement-in-education.pdf

5. Much of the research on overparenting has been conducted among college students: Terri LeMoyne and Tom Buchanan, "Does 'Hovering' Matter? Helicopter Parenting and Its Effect on Well-Being," *Sociological Spectrum*, 31 (2011): 399–418.

6. Bruce D. Baker, David G. Sciarra, and Danielle Farrie, "Is School Funding Fair? A National Report Card," 3rd ed., January 2014 (Newark, NJ: Education Law Center, 2014), http://www.schoolfundingfairness.org/National_Report_Card_2014.pdf

7. Baker et al., "Is School Funding Fair?," 15.

8. Michael Leachman and Chris Mai, *Most States Funding Schools Less Than Before the Recession*, Center on Budget and Policy Priorities, revised May 20, 2014, http://www.cbpp.org/cms/?fa=view&id=4011

9. Frederick Mosteller, "The Tennessee Study of Class Size in the Early School Grades," *The Future of Children, Critical Issues for Children and Youths*, 5 (1995): 113–127; Barbara Nye, Larry Hedges, and Spyros Konstantopoulos, "The Effects of Small Classes on Academic Achievement: The Results of the Tennessee Class Size Experiment," *American Educational Research Journal*, 37 (2000): 123–151.

10. OECD, *TALIS 2013 Results: Country Note, United States*, July 2013, http://www.oecd.org/unitedstates/TALIS-2013-country-note-US.pdf

11. Eliah Watlington, Robert Shockley, Paul Guglielmino, and Rivka Felsher, "The High Cost of Leaving: An Analysis of the Cost of Teacher Turnover," *Journal of Education Finance*, 36 (2010): 22–37.

12. "On the Path to Equity: Improving the Effectiveness of Beginning Teachers," Alliance for Excellent Education, July 2014, http://all4ed.org/wp-content/uploads/2014/07/PathToEquity.pdf

13. Richard M. Ingersoll, "Teacher Turnover and Teacher Shortages: An Organizational Analysis," *American Educational Research Journal*, 38 (2001): 499–534.

14. Richard M. Ingersoll, "Why Do Schools Have Difficulty Staffing Their Classrooms with Qualified Teachers?" (testimony for September 10, 2013, hearing in the Pennsylvania House of Representatives), http://www.legis.state.pa.us/cfdocs/legis/TR/transcripts/2013_0167_0001_TSTMNY.pdf

15. Nicole Leinbach-Reyhle, "Teachers Spend Their Own Money on Back to School Supplies," *Forbes.com*, August 19, 2014.

16. Arizona Education Association, *Changes in Arizona Teacher and Principal Evaluations*, 2011, http://www.arizonaea.org/home/319.htm

Chapter 7

1. Roberto Alvarez Jr., "The Lemon Grove Incident: The Nation's First Successful Desegregation Court Case," *The Journal of San Diego History*, 32 (1986): 1.

2. The National Alliance for Public Charter Schools, *The Public Schools Dashboard, Figures for 2012–2013*, 2014, http://dashboard.publiccharters.org/dashboard/schools/page/overview/year/2013

3. The figure is from 2009–2010. The National Alliance for Public Charter Schools, *The Public Schools Dashboard*, 2014, http://dashboard.publiccharters.org/dashboard/schools/page/union/year/2014; the Bureau of Labor Statistics gives a figure of 15% but does not disaggregate K–12 teachers from instructors at all levels. Bureau of Labor Statistics, U.S. Department of Labor, "Table 3: Union Affiliation of Employed Wage and Salary Workers by Occupation and Industry," *Economic News Release January 24, 2014*, http://www.bls.gov/news.release/union2.t03.htm

4. The National Alliance for Public Charter Schools, *The Public Schools Dashboard*, 2014, http://dashboard.publiccharters.org/dashboard/schools/page/elt/year/2014

5. The mean base teaching salary of regular full-time charter schoolteachers is $44,500 compared with $53,400 for traditional public school teachers. Rebecca Goldring, Lucinda Gray, and Amy Bitterman, *Characteristics of Public and Elementary and Secondary School Teachers in the United States*, National Center for Education Statistics, August 2013, http://nces.ed.gov/pubs2013/2013314.pdf

6. Betheny Gross, *Inside Charter Schools: Unlocking Doors to Student Success*, Center on Reinventing Public Education: National Charter School Research

Project, February 2011, http://www.crpe.org/sites/default/files/pub_ICS_ Unlock_Feb11_0.pdf

7. See Henry A. Giroux, *Corporate Culture and the Attack on Higher Education and Public School* (Bloomington, IN: Phi Delta Kappa Educational Foundation Fastback Series, 1999).

8. "Charter Discipline: The Impact on Students," *Education Week*, February 20, 2014, http://www.edweek.org/ew/collections/charter-discipline/

9. "Charter Discipline."

10. Bernard Weiner, "Attribution Theory, Achievement, Motivation and the Educational Process," *Review of Educational Research*, 42 (1972): 203–215.

11. The National Alliance for Public Charter Schools, *The Public Schools Dashboard*, http://dashboard.publiccharters.org/dashboard/schools/page/ locale/year/2012

12. Many education historians point to the emergence of magnet schools during the period following *Brown v. Board of Education* as the beginning of the public school choice movement. Christine Rossell, "Magnet Schools," *Education Next*, Spring 2005, 44–49, http://educationnext.org/ files/ednext20052_44.pdf; a foundation text for this movement is Milton Friedman's essay "The Role of Government in Education," in *Capitalism and Freedom* (Chicago: University of Chicago Press, 1962), http://site.ebrary. com/lib/alltitles/docDetail.action?docID=10275474&ppg=102

13. The National Alliance for Public Charter Schools, *The Public Schools Dashboard*, http://dashboard.publiccharters.org/dashboard/students/page/ race/year/2012

14. Erica Frankenberg and Genevieve Siegel-Hawley, *Equity Overlooked: Charter Schools and Civil Rights Policy*, Civil Rights Project, November 1, 2009; W. Parker, "From the Failure of Desegregation to the Failure of Choice," *Washington University Journal of Law and Policy*, 40 (2012), http://digitalcommons. law.wustl.edu/cgi/viewcontent.cgi?article=1578&context=wujlp

15. Jonathan C. Augustine, "America's New Civil Rights Movement: Education Reform, Public Charter Schools, and No Child Left Behind," *Louisiana Bar Journal*, 59 (2012): 340–343, http://papers.ssrn.com/sol3/ papers.cfm?abstract_id=2021316

16. Teach Plus Working Group on Public Charter Schools, "Why Are My Teachers Leaving?" Teach Plus, 2012, http://www.teachplus.org/uploads/ Documents/1340224253_WhyAreMyTeachersLeaving062012.pdf

17. The Center for Popular Democracy and the Alliance for Quality Education, "Risking Public Money: New York Charter School Fraud: Best Practices to Protect Public Dollars and Prevent Financial Mismanagement," November 2014, http://populardemocracy.org/sites/default/files/CPD_ AQE_Charter-Schools-NewYork-Report.pdf

18. The Opportunity to Learn Campaign, Framework for Providing All Students an Opportunity to Learn Through Reauthorization of

the Elementary and Secondary Education Act, July 2010, http://www.otlcampaign.org/sites/default/files/resources/CivilRights%20framework-FINAL.7-25-10.pdf

19. Fifty-three percent of the student body in the larger high school district to which the school belongs is White, but no school data are publicly available for Liberty Charter High School–the only data available are for the aggregate of Liberty Charter's schools. These data show the four schools as enrolling 49% non-Hispanic Whites.

20. Sean F. Reardon, Elena Grewal, Demetra Kalogrides, and Erica Greenberg, "Brown Fades: The End of Court-Ordered School Desegregation and the Resegregation of American Public Schools," *Journal of Policy Analysis and Management*, 31 (2012): 876–904.

21. Alvarez, "The Lemon Grove Incident."

22. Alvarez, "The Lemon Grove Incident."

Chapter 8

1. Jeffrey Ostler, *The Plains Sioux and U.S. Colonialism from Lewis and Clark to Wounded Knee* (Cambridge, UK: Cambridge University Press, 2004).

2. U.S. Department of the Interior, Office of the Secretary, Office of the Assistant Secretary–Indian Affairs, *2013 American Indian Population and Labor Force Report* (Washington, DC: U.S. Department of the Interior, February 2014), 47.

3. Oglala Lakota College, accessed June 14, 2014, http://www.olc.edu/

4. Little Wound High School, accessed June 14, 2014, http://www.littlewound.us/

5. Little Wound High School, accessed June 14, 2014, http://www.littlewound.us/

6. Alex Molnar, ed., *Virtual Schools in the U.S. 2014: Politics, Performance, Policy, and Research Evidence* (Boulder, CO: National Education Policy Center, March 2014); John Watson, Amy Murin, Lauren Vashaw, Butch Gemin, and Chris Rapp, "Keeping Pace with K–12 Online and Blended Learning: An Annual Review of Policy and Practice (2013)," Evergreen Education Group, http://kpk12.com/cms/wp-content/uploads/EEG_KP2013-lr.pdf

7. Lisa Plummer, "Assuring a Virtual Second Chance," *T H E Journal*, 39 (2012): 20–22.

8. Alyson Klein and Lesli A. Maxwell, "Federal Cuts Take a Toll on Native Americans' Schools: Sequestration's Impact Is Disproportionate," *Education Week*, December 4, 2013, http://www.edweek.org/ew/articles/2013/12/04/13sequestration_ep.h33.html

9. James Ainsworth, ed., *Sociology of Education: An A to Z Guide* (Thousand Oaks, CA: Sage, 2013), 78–79.

10. "Diplomas Count–Motivation Matters: Engaging Students, Creating Learners," *Education Week*, June 2014.

11. Ronica Arnold Branson, "A Pilot Study: An Exploration of Social, Emotional, and Academic Factors Influencing School Dropout," *Researcher: An Interdisciplinary Journal*, 26 (2013): 1–17.

12. Sherry L. Murphy, Jiaquan Xu, and Kenneth D. Kochanek, "Deaths: Final Data for 2010," Centers for Disease Control and Prevention, May 8, 2013, http://www.cdc.gov/nchs/data/nvsr/nvsr61/nvsr61_04.pdf

13. U.S. Department of Education, "Promoting Grit, Tenacity, and Perseverance: Critical Factors for Success in the 21st Century" (draft), February 14, 2013, http://www.ed.gov/edblogs/technology/files/2013/02/OET-Draft-Grit-Report-2-17-13.pdf

14. Camille A. Farrington, Melissa Roderick, Elaine Allensworth, Jenny Nagaoka, Tasha Seneca Keyes, David W. Johnson, and Nicole O. Beechum, *Teaching Adolescents to Become Learners: The Role of Noncognitive Factors in Shaping School Performance; A Critical Literature Review* (Chicago: University of Chicago Consortium on Chicago School Research, 2012), https://ccsr.uchicago.edu/sites/default/files/publications/Noncognitive%20Report.pdf

15. Richard Rothstein, Class and Schools: Using Social, Economic, and Educational Reform to Close the Black–White Achievement Gap (Washington, DC: Economic Policy Institute, 2004).

16. U.S. Department of the Interior, Office of the Secretary, Office of the Assistant Secretary–Indian Affairs, "2013 American Indian Population and Labor Force Report" (Washington, DC: Department of the Interior, 2014), 47.

17. Oglala Lakota College, accessed June 14, 2014, http://www.olc.edu/

Chapter 9

1. Despite recent school shootings, American children are physically much safer at school than elsewhere. Homicides of children in school represent a tiny percentage of the total (less than 2% in 2010). Children are far likelier to be killed being driven to or from school by a parent than they are to be killed in school. Centers for Disease Control and Prevention, "Deaths: Leading Causes for 2010," *National Vital Statistics Report* 62, no. 6, http://www.cdc.gov/nchs/products/nvsr.htm

2. 2012 estimate. "State and County Quick Facts: Palatine, Illinois," United States Census Bureau, last modified June 11, 2014, accessed June 29, 2014, http://quickfacts.census.gov/qfd/states/17/1757225.html

3. Suniya S. Luthar and Shawn J. Latendresse, "Children of the Affluent: Challenges to Well-Being," *Current Directions in Psychological Science*, 14 (2005): 49–53.

4. Alison King, "From Sage on the Stage to Guide on the Side," *College Teaching*, 41 (1993): 30–35.

5. At the start of the 2013–2014 school year, 70% of teens aged 13–17 owned a smartphone. "Ring the Bells: More Smartphones in Students' Hands Ahead of Back-to-School Season," *Nielsen*, October 29, 2013, http://

www.nielsen.com/us/en/newswire/2013/ring-the-bells-more-smartphones-in-students-hands-ahead-of-back.html

6. Dewey G. Cornell and Matthew J. Mayer, "Why Do School Order and Safety Matter?" *Educational Researcher*, 39 (2010): 7–15.

7. Julianne C. Turner, "The Influence of Classroom Contexts on Young Children's Motivation for Literacy," *Reading Research Quarterly*, 30 (1995): 410–441.

8. Common Core State Standards Initiative, "English Language Arts Standards," http://www.corestandards.org/ELA-Literacy/

9. NAEP, National Center for Education Statistics, 2013 Mathematics and Reading: Grade 12 Assessments, "Are the Nation's Twelfth-Graders Making Progress in Mathematics and Reading?" http://nationsreportcard.gov/reading_math_g12_2013/#/

10. Victoria J. Rideout, Ulla G. Foehr, and Donald F. Roberts, "Generation M2: Media in the Lives of 8- to 18-Year-Olds," Henry J. Kaiser Family Foundation, January 20, 2010, http://kff.org/other/report/generation-m2-media-in-the-lives-of-8-to-18-year-olds/

11. Jacob Lowell Bishop and Matthew A. Verleger, "The Flipped Classroom: A Survey of the Research," 2013 ASEE Annual Conference, June 23–26, 2013, http://www.asee.org/public/conferences/20/papers/6219/view

12. Michael S. Garet, Andrew C. Porter, Laura Desimone, Beatrice F. Birman, and Kwang Suk Yoon, "What Makes Professional Development Effective? Analysis of a National Sample of Teachers," *American Education Research Journal*, 38 (2001): 915–945; Ellen Behrstock-Sherratt, Katherine Bassett, Derk Olson, and Catherine Jacques, *From Good to Great: Exemplary Teachers Share Perspectives on Increasing Teacher Effectiveness Across the Career Continuum* (Washington, DC: American Institutes for Research, April 2014), http://www.gtlcenter.org/sites/default/files/Good_to_Great_Report.pdf

index

about the authors

Anne Lutz Fernandez has been teaching English in Connecticut public middle and high schools for 15 years. Prior to this, she was a consumer products executive and an investment banker with Credit Suisse First Boston, where she was chief operating officer of the Merger & Acquisition Group. She sits on the scholarship selection committee for the Gordon A. Rich Memorial Foundation. Anne holds a BA in political science from Brown University and a master's in teaching English from Boston College. She is the author, with Catherine Lutz, of *Carjacked: The Culture of the Automobile and Its Effect on Our Lives.* Her writing has appeared in *The Boston Globe, The Guardian (UK),* and elsewhere.

Catherine Lutz is the Thomas J. Watson Jr. Family Professor at Brown University. Past president of the American Ethnological Society, she has received numerous honors and awards, including, most recently, a John Simon Guggenheim Fellowship. She is the author of a number of books about the United States and its cultures, including *Reading National Geographic* with Jane L. Collins and *Homefront: A Military City and the American 20th Century.* Her editorials, articles, and book reviews have appeared in *The New York Times, The Los Angeles Times, The New Statesman,* and *The Nation,* among other publications.